AF574386

100 THINGS TO DO IN COLORADO SPRINGS BEFORE YOU DIE

5/4/19

Jake—
travel local & enjoy!
Best,
Kirsten Akens

Mesa Overlook
(Credit: Kirsten Akens)

100 THINGS TO DO IN COLORADO SPRINGS BEFORE YOU DIE

KIRSTEN AKENS

Reedy Press
PO Box 5131
St. Louis, MO 63139, USA
www.reedypress.com

Library of Congress Control Number: 1681061961

ISBN: 9781681061962

Design by Jill Halpin

Cover Photo: Garden of the Gods *(Credit: Jenny Kruckeberg)*

Author Photo: Kirsten Akens (*Credit: Rebecca Tillett*)

Printed in the United States of America
19 20 21 22 23   5 4 3 2 1

Please note that websites, phone numbers, addresses, and company names are subject to change or cancellation. We did our best to relay the most accurate information available, but due to circumstances beyond our control, please do not hold us liable for misinformation. When exploring new destinations, please do your homework before you go.

CONTENTS

Arts and Entertainment

Sports and Recreation

Culture and History

Shopping and Fashion

PREFACE

I'm not a Colorado Springs native. I arrived here more than twenty-five years ago, a bright-eyed eighteen-year-old starting my first semester at Colorado College. The city's population was smaller then, downtown a bit more quiet, and the north end not so far north. Overall, though, the range of arts, culture, dining, shopping, and outdoor activities throughout the Pikes Peak region was impressive—even for someone who grew up outside of Chicago.

Since then, the population has almost doubled. According to the United States Census Bureau's 2017 estimates, we're nearing half a million residents. The city's location at the base of Pikes Peak makes it an easy natural playground for hikers, mountain bikers, rock climbers, wildlife and wildflower photographers, and more. But it's also a stunning environment for those who prefer to relax with one of our famous Colorado craft brews in hand, wander the innovative and interactive public art all over downtown, or meet Team USA athletes while touring the United States Olympic Training Center.

I like to think the Springs is a bit of a hidden gem, often overlooked by potential tourists and residents alike for larger cities. But in 2018, *U.S. News and World Report* rated Colorado

Springs the Most Desirable Place to Live in the United States, so I guess the secret's out.

Within this book, I'll share a bit of our region with you, from iconic locations like Garden of the Gods and the US Air Force Academy, to the lesser-known people, places, and activities here, such as our TV-celebrity chefs, AAA Five-Diamond resort, and National Museum for World War II Aviation.

Twenty-three million people visit Colorado Springs each year. Perhaps this book will inspire you to do the same. And if you're already in the region, passing through or permanently, thanks for reading! I hope this book encourages you, as writing it did me, to get out and dig into this fun, captivating, and welcoming community.

Kirsten Akens

ACKNOWLEDGMENTS

Thanks and gratitude to . . .

PK Knickerbocker and Pikes Peak Country Attractions (pikes-peak.com), and Claire Swinford and the Downtown Partnership of Colorado Springs (downtowncs.com) for answering a multitude of questions and helping me make connections.

Amber S., Ann, Cari, Janet, Jessica, JL, Joy, Kirk, Kitty, Matthew, Melanie, Michele, and Zach for your support and enthusiasm.

Mom and Dad, for impressing upon me at a very young age the fun and value of traveling and experiencing everything around me, near and far (even though I spent many a road trip car sick in the back seat).

Geoff, for playing along when I asked repeatedly, "Did you know that . . .?", for listening to and loving me, and for being my partner on this trip called life.

Credit: Jon Collins

FOOD AND DRINK

1

DINE AT SHUGA'S AND MORE
IN THE DOWNTOWN CORE

There are many reasons Shuga's has spent a lot of time on Yelp as the No. 1 restaurant in Colorado Springs, with a 4.5-star rating and nearly one thousand reviews.

The food is the first reason, from the spicy Brazilian shrimp soup to the Nicoise salad to the almond butter cake. The beverages are the second, including creative, seasonal cocktails and the übertasty lemon-ginger tea. The friendly staff is third, and fourth is the space itself, a restored 1910 grocery store on the south edge of downtown, often with local art on the walls and folded paper cranes hanging from the ceiling.

Visit Shuga's for lunch, dinner, drinks, weekly film screenings, live music, and a warm fuzzy feeling inside.

Shuga's
702 S. Cascade Ave., Colorado Springs
719-328-1412, shugas.com

Downtown and have a specific food craving? There's a good chance one of the many restaurants can fill that need. Here's a small sampling of local favorites with different flavors to try.

Coquette's Bistro and Bakery
100 percent gluten-free
616 S. Tejon St., Colorado Springs
719-685-2420, coquettesbistro.com

Il Vicino
Wood-oven pizza
11 S. Tejon St., Colorado Springs
719-475-9224, ilvicino.com

Mediterranean Café
Greek
118 E. Kiowa St., Colorado Springs
719-633-0115, medcafe-co.com

Saigon Café
Vietnamese
20 E. Colorado Ave., Colorado Springs
719-633-2888, coloradosaigoncafe.com

Sonterra Grill
Southwest
28B S. Tejon St., Colorado Springs
719-471-9222, sonterragrill.com

StreetCar 520
Globally inspired menu
520 S. Tejon St., Colorado Springs
719-633-3300, streetcar520.com

Wild Goose Meeting House
Café
401 N. Tejon St., Colorado Springs
719-445-0170, wildgoosemeetinghouse.com

2

ENJOY DINNER AND A MOVIE UNDER THE STARS

AT MARGARITA AT PINE CREEK

Summer isn't summer in the Springs until you're sitting at a patio table at Margarita at Pine Creek on a Friday evening in June waiting for dusk. As stars start to twinkle overhead, servers lower the outdoor movie screen above the bar, and that week's feature film begins. Weekly through September, Margarita pairs flicks from *Rear Window* to *La La Land* with local, organic dishes like griddled chorizo tacos and lamb merguez flatbread. After selecting an entrée, or the forty-three-year-old restaurant's five-course prix fixe option, your most difficult decision will be whether to pair a lemon-cucumber cooler, a house-infused ginger lime martini, or a Bristol Brewing Company beer with the complimentary popcorn passed around as the opening credits roll.

Margarita at Pine Creek
7350 Pine Creek Rd., Colorado Springs
719-598-8667, margaritaatpinecreek.com

GO BACK TO SCHOOL
FOR DINNER, DRINKS, AND DONUTS

Bookending the north and south ends of downtown Colorado Springs are two reimagined and refurbished former elementary schools.

At the south, Ivywild School became the first community marketplace of its type locally in 2013. That's when the domineering structure that had been built in 1916 and that closed as a school in 2009 was reopened with anchor Bristol Brewery and Pub. Alongside Bristol, the space now features coffee and cocktails in The Principal's Office, comfort food by Old School Bakery, local bourbon from The Axe and The Oak, and ethically sourced craft goods at Yobel Market.

At the north, Lincoln Elementary, which closed in 2015, became Lincoln Center a year later. It's home to more than fifteen vendors, including Goat Patch Brewing Company, Red Point Café, Building 3 Coffee Roasters, and the absolutely not-to-miss craft bake shop, Nightingale Bread.

Ivywild School
1604 S. Cascade Ave., Colorado Springs
719-368-6100, ivywildschool.com

Lincoln Center
2727 N. Cascade Ave., Colorado Springs
lincolncenter-cosprings.com

4

GRAB A MEAL, OR THREE,
IN MANITOU SPRINGS

Adam's Mountain Café is one of those rare places where a person—and a vegetarian at that—could eat three meals over the course of one day and have absolutely no regrets except a tight belt.

Start with a breakfast of orange almond French toast and the house orange spice tea. Grab a Small Planet Burger or Harvest Crepes for lunch. Finish your evening with an appetizer of crostini with figs and pears and the Rural Italian Lasagna as your main.

Of course, don't just take our word for it. Ask around. Every local we know has lots of favorite items at Adam's, many of which have been on the menu since the vegetarian-forward restaurant opened in 1985.

Adam's Mountain Café
26 Manitou Ave., Manitou Springs
719-685-1430, adamsmountaincafe.com

For such a small town, Manitou features lots of great locally owned restaurants. Try some of these other options.

Cliff House Dining Room
AAA Four Diamond restaurant for those fancy nights out
306 Cañon Ave., Manitou Springs
719-785-2415, thecliffhouse.com

Crystal Park Cantina
Home-style Mexican, owned by former
Denver Broncos football player Justin Armour
178 Crystal Park Rd., Manitou Springs
719-685-5999, crystalparkcantina.com

Good Karma Café
Breakfast, lunch, coffee, and tasty baked goods
110 Cañon Ave., Suite A, Manitou Springs, 719-685-2325

The Loop
Come for the margaritas, stay for the margaritas
965 Manitou Ave., Manitou Springs
719-685-9344, theloopatmanitou.com

The Mona Lisa
Bring your appetite for a four-course fondue extravaganza
733 Manitou Ave., Manitou Springs
719-685-0277, monalisafondue.com

Sahara Café
Tasty Middle Eastern food
954 Manitou Ave., Manitou Springs
719-685-2303, thesaharacafe.com

Swirl Wine Bar
Come for the wine, stay for the wine and the food
717 Manitou Ave., Manitou Springs
719-685-2294, swirlismybar.com

5

SAY "SÌ" TO PIZZA, PASTA, AND FAMILY

AT ROMAN VILLA

Raise a glass of Chianti and send up an enthusiastic toast to Roman Villa. One of the longest-running family-owned restaurants in Colorado Springs, the Villa celebrates its sixtieth anniversary in 2019. Four generations have perfected the original recipes still served today. Chicago-style thin-crust pizza. Handmade ravioli. Chicken cacciatore. The cheesy, spinachy, creamy, stuffed-pasta dish known as tortellacci.

There's no wrong choice at Roman Villa—and there's a good chance your dinner will be served up by a family member or two. That same family member may also be the one to unlock the door at 5:00 p.m., to welcome in the line of people typically waiting out front for dinner service (Tuesday through Saturday only) to begin.

Roman Villa
3005 N. Nevada Ave., Colorado Springs
719-635-1806, romanvillaonline.weebly.com

Roman Villa isn't the only local restaurant with history. Here are six others that have been around at least four decades.

Edelweiss
German, opened 1967
34 E. Ramona Ave., Colorado Springs
719-633-2220, edelweissrest.com

El Taco Rey
Mexican, opened 1976
330 E. Colorado Ave., Colorado Springs
719-475-9722, eltacorey.com

Fargo's
Pizza in an Old West-style restaurant, opened 1973
2910 E. Platte Ave., Colorado Springs
719-473-5540, fargospizza.com

Juniper Valley Ranch
Family-style chicken dinners, opened 1951
16350 Hwy. 115, Colorado Springs
719-576-0741, junipervalleyranch.com

Luigi's
Italian, opened 1958
947 S. Tejon St., Colorado Springs
719-632-7339, luigiscoloradosprings.com

Panino's
Italian, opened 1974
604 N. Tejon St., Colorado Springs, 719-635-7452
1721 S. Eighth St., Colorado Springs, 719-635-1188
3015 New Center Point, Colorado Springs, 719-380-2720
paninos.com

DISH UP FOOD AND MUCH MORE
AT POOR RICHARD'S

It doesn't matter which of four doors off Tejon Street you choose to enter Poor Richard's. Though each door opens into a different concept, everything's connected inside.

Start in Poor Richard's Restaurant, one of the original components opened by owner Richard Skorman in 1977. Step up to the counter and order Pizza Meal Deal No. 1, for a solid sampling of the food here. It includes a three-topping thin-crust pizza slice and a small-but-loaded house salad with the best balsamic dressing in town.

Hit Rico's Café and Wine Bar for an Americano or a glass of cab, and most evenings enjoy it alongside local live music. After eating and sipping, peruse Poor Richard's Books and Gifts for new and used titles, and a bevy of locally made jewelry, cards, and other unique handcrafted items.

Finally, while it may be tempting to send the kids alone to Little Richard's Toy Store, you'll miss out if you do. It's packed with fun and creative products for all ages.

Poor Richard's
320-324½ N. Tejon St., Colorado Springs
719-578-5549, poorrichardsdowntown.com

7

TASTE A WHOLE LOT
OF COLORADO WINES

Colorado is home to some of the highest-altitude vineyards in the world, and 90 percent of the state's winemaking grapes are still grown on the Western Slope where winemaking began more than one hundred years ago.

Visitors don't have to go that far from the Springs, however, to access most of the wines produced. Wines of Colorado, located in Cascade at the turnoff for Pikes Peak Highway, offers a selection of free tastings aside glass and bottle sales of wines from the more than ninety-five wineries represented. Don't just stop to sip some tasters though; the cozy, creek-side Wines of Colorado restaurant serves up full lunch and dinner menus, including mouth-watering wine, buffalo, or portobello mushroom burgers fresh from the grill.

Wines of Colorado
8045 W. Hwy. 24, Cascade
719-684-0900, winesofcolorado.com

8

TAKE HIGH TEA
AT MIRAMONT CASTLE

Tours at Miramont Castle introduce visitors to the nine architectural styles that Father Jean Baptiste Francolon employed when he began to build the structure in 1895. It's worth exploring the random blend of Moorish, English Tudor, Romanesque, and more.

But to spend some quality time and enjoy a Victorian-style meal at the Castle, make a mid-day reservation with friends and family at the Queen's Parlour Victorian Tearoom. Miramont serves a four-course high tea, a three-course light tea, a crème tea, a prince or princess tea for the kids, and individual items from a lunch menu. Very, very civilized!

Miramont Castle
9 Capitol Hill Ave., Manitou Springs
719-685-1011, miramontcastle.org

9

TOAST THE WORLD'S BEST RYE WHISKEY AT DISTILLERY 291

Colorado Springs may not seem like the obvious location for an award-winning whiskey producer. And yet, in 2018, *Whisky Magazine* honored Distillery 291's Single Barrel Colorado Rye Whiskey not only as the Best American Rye, but as the World's Best Rye.

It's not the only award that 291's whiskies have won since owner Michael Myers opened in 2011, but it's definitely the biggest nod to his success. He describes his 2018 winner as uniquely "Wild West whiskey"—a rye that's a bit spicy, a bit hot, and finished with aspen staves. Sample this award-winner as a part of the eight-flagship-whiskey flight at 291's tasting room and grab a bottle to share (or not) with friends and family.

Distillery 291
1647 S. Tejon St., Colorado Springs
719-323-8010, distillery291.com

10

DRINK CRAFT BEER
AT LOCAL BREWPUBS

About 10 percent of Colorado's 350 craft breweries reside in the Pikes Peak region. The largest locally is Bristol Brewing Company. Bristol brews and serves up flagship and seasonal beers such as Laughing Lab Scottish Ale in the former elementary classrooms of Ivywild School.

The oldest craft brewery is Phantom Canyon Brewing Company, with fifteen brews regularly on tap and a phenomenal beer cheese soup on the food menu. Speaking of eats, Cerberus Brewing Company, a former animal hospital that welcomes dogs on its patio, receives as many accolades for its cuisine as its tap.

The brewmasters at Paradox Beer Company, in Divide, barrel-age and bottle-condition every beer they produce. And the veteran-owned Red Leg Brewing Company honors the large active duty and retired military community here in the company and in beer names as well as in its can designs.

Bristol Brewing Co.
1604 S. Cascade Ave., Colorado Springs
719-633-2555, bristolbrewing.com

Phantom Canyon Brewing Co.
2 E. Pikes Peak Ave., Colorado Springs
719-635-2800, phantomcanyon.com

Cerberus Brewing Co.
702 W. Colorado Ave., Colorado Springs
719-636-2337, cerberusbrewingco.com

Paradox Beer Co.
10 Buffalo Ct., Divide
719-686-8081, paradoxbeercompany.com

Red Leg Brewing Co.
4630 Forge Rd., Suite B, Colorado Springs
719-598-3776, redlegbrewing.com

11

SAVOR BIG FLAVORS
IN THIS TINY HOUSE COFFEE SHOP

Even though the food-truck industry continues to grow here and across the country, downtown Acacia Park is home to what still might be the only tiny house coffee shop in the world.

Step inside Story Coffee Company, and let your mouth gape open. Not only does one wall of floor-to-ceiling windows make the 160-square-foot interior feel bigger than it is, but the clean, minimalistic lines, high-top tables, and shiny silver espresso machine encourage sitting, sipping, and chatting with whoever is working the bar. If it's owners Don or Carissa Niemyer, they'll likely ask for your story along with your order. The two—whose personal tale includes living in a hundred-square-foot VW Rialta with their kids for almost four years before opening Story—are very passionate about understanding their coffee and their customers.

Story Coffee Co.
120 E. Bijou St., Colorado Springs
503-758-4444, storycoffeecompany.com

TIP

Story roasts its own beans, and locals love the Palmer Blend, which gives a nod to the city's founder. If you're looking for a fun Springs-themed gift, Story isn't the only local roaster to glean inspiration from its hometown. Others to try: Institute Street from Switchback Coffee Roasters (switchbackroasters.com) and 1918, Old Stage Road, or Ute Pass from Ümpire Estate Mountain Roasters sold by Colorado Coffee Merchants (facebook.com/umpireestate).

12

EAT VEGAN
IN THE SPRINGS

Just five years ago, 100-percent-vegan restaurants were nonexistent in Colorado Springs. As the community has grown, so have the options. Vegans and non-vegans alike now frequent five spots.

Burrowing Owl is a chill westside neighborhood lounge with traditional bar food done vegan and the most inexpensive creative cocktails in the city. Moxie, the plant-based, fine-dining option, offers appetizers, entrées, and craft cocktails that compete with bigger cities' vegan fare.

Santana's Vegan Grill meets every vegan's fast-food, drive-thru cravings for grilled "burgers," "hot dogs," and "chicken" sliders. Finally, Ola Juice Bar, owned by the Moxie folks, and Nourish Organic Juice both serve up organic juices, smoothies, salads, and other house specialties. But keep an eye out, because they both use honey in certain items.

Burrowing Owl
1791 S. Eighth St., Colorado Springs
719-434-3864, burrowingowllounge.com

Moxie
925 S. Eighth St., Colorado Springs
719-465-3595, livemoxie.co

Santana's Vegan Grill
3220 Austin Bluffs Pkwy., Colorado Springs
719-271-9113, santanasvegangrill.com

Ola Juice Bar
27 E. Kiowa St., Colorado Springs
719-633-3111, olajuicebar.com

Nourish Organic Juice
303 E. Pikes Peak Ave., Colorado Springs
719-634-5686, nourishorganicjuice.com

13

GET BUZZED
AT THE GOLDEN BEE

Be forewarned. When you walk into The Broadmoor's Golden Bee, a server will flick a bee at you. And *flick a bee* isn't some sort of euphemism.

Since the 1980s, employees have become quite talented at tossing dime-sized embroidered bee stickers onto guests' shirts, purses, or bald heads when they arrive for a drink or a meal at the resort's nineteenth-century British pub. It's a sign of the fun to come, which includes sipping ale from traditional yard glasses while chowing down on fish and chips, singing along with the ragtime piano player, and learning the story of the pub's transport from the United Kingdom and panel-by-panel reconstruction in the Springs.

The Broadmoor's Golden Bee
1 Lake Ave., Colorado Springs
719-577-5733, broadmoor.com/dining/golden-bee

14

EVERYONE SCREAMS
FOR JOSH & JOHN'S ICE CREAM

Josh & John's Ice Cream has got local award-winning on repeat—partly because it's dang tasty, but also because the owners have put many years into perfecting its product. After graduating from Colorado College in 1985, John Krakauer made a home here and, with high school friend Josh Paris, dreamed up the best ice cream shop possible.

J&J's ice cream stays on top thanks to its unique-to-Colorado slow-churn process in turn-of-the-century rock salt and ice freezers. While you wait in line, watch the churning as it happens in the front windows at the original downtown location and try to decide among the more than fifteen flavors. (Tip: You can never go wrong with Oatmeal Cookie—unless you're gluten-free. If so, you've got eight other options.)

Josh & John's Ice Cream
111 E. Pikes Peak Ave., Colorado Springs, 719-632-0299
6896 Centennial Blvd., Colorado Springs, 719-532-0299
2710 North Gate Blvd., Colorado Springs, 719-203-6729
joshandjohns.com

15

HUNT DOWN FOOD TRUCKS

ON THE GO

The many food trucks in Colorado Springs haven't been able to find a permanent hub, but they're still out there doing their mobile thing, serving up dishes-to-go at brewpubs, art openings, and special events like the Downtown Partnership's summer lunchtime Food Truck Tuesdays outside the Colorado Springs Pioneers Museum.

The best way to track them down is to poke around online, give them a call for their weekly calendars, or simply hit the brakes (carefully) when you see a parked and open-for-business truck. Especially worth hitting the breaks for are Potato Potato (loaded fries, specialty poutine, potato-based soups), PigLatin (Latin American flavors), and Gold Star Pies (sweet pie slices, neat or à la mode).

Potato Potato, 719-362-0750
facebook.com/potatopotatocos

PigLatin, 719-347-1144
facebook.com/PigLatinTruck

Gold Star Pies, 719-447-5219
goldstarpies.com

16

FIND EVERYTHING FRESH, INDOORS AND OUTDOORS,

AT LOCAL MARKETS

During the summer and early fall months, outdoor farmers markets flourish across the Pikes Peak region, offering everything from local honey and Colorado's famous peaches to fancy breads and specialty cheeses.

Two of the largest and most well-known are the Pikes Peak Farmers Market on Saturdays in Old Colorado City and the Colorado Farm and Art Market on Wednesday evenings at Pioneers Museum and Saturday mornings at Margarita at Pine Creek.

The newest to the area, however, is the year-round indoor Pikes Peak Market, a nonprofit public market that is both a hub for local food and craft artisans to share their wares and a community space for open mics, book signings, and salsa lessons.

Pikes Peak Farmers Market
pikespeakfarmersmarket.com

Colorado Farm and Art Market
farmandartmarket.com

Pikes Peak Market, 315 E. Pikes Peak Ave., Colorado Springs
719-337-9676, pikespeakmarket.com

17

APPRECIATE AUTHENTIC ETHIOPIAN
AT UCHENNA

Uchenna owner Maya Hetman doesn't just make the best dishes from her native Ethiopian recipes; she also gives the best hugs. And once you've entered her restaurant, you become like family. So there's no escaping her arms enfolding you or saying anything but yes.

Say yes to the rose-water lemonade. Say yes to a combo plate to taste the red lentils, the collard greens, and the chickpeas, all cooked up in exotic spices. And say yes to eating with your fingers because it's the authentic way. Use the slightly sour, 100 percent teff flour injera bread to soak up the tiniest bits so you can get every one of them into your oh-so-satisfied mouth.

Uchenna
2501 W. Colorado Ave., Suite 105, Colorado Springs
719-634-5070, uchennaalive.com

Truth be told, about twenty-five locally owned restaurants call Old Colorado City home, and none of them is a bad choice. So pick what your taste buds crave, or try another one of our personal favorites listed here.

Front Range Barbeque
2330 W. Colorado Ave., Colorado Springs
719-632-2596, frbbq.com

Jake and Telly's Greek Taverna
2616 W. Colorado Ave., Colorado Springs
719-633-0406, jakeandtellys.com

La Baguette and The Wine Bar Upstairs at La Baguette
2417 W. Colorado Ave., Colorado Springs
719-577-4818, labaguette-co.com

Pizzeria Rustica
2527 W. Colorado Ave., Colorado Springs
719-632-8121, pizzeriarustica.com

18

SAMPLE COCKTAILS
WITH A BUDDY

Cocktails are cool on their own, but pair them with something unexpected for a special treat. Want cocktails and coffee? Hit Loyal Coffee for the Draft Coffee Beer or an Ole Smoky with coffee-infused mezcal. For cocktails with prohibition-era style, visit Brooklyn's on Boulder. The "fine haberdashery" makes the getting in to the speakeasy challenging but the sipping simple.

For cocktails and waffles, drop by Urban Steam and pair a loaded Bloody Hairy with a strawberry-topped Waffle-Waffle. Finally, find cocktails, sushi, and cyberpunk at Chiba Bar, and order up the Sashimi Donburi Bowl with a side of sake, Yamazaki 12 neat, or gin-based Lychee Buck.

Loyal Coffee
408 S. Nevada Ave., Colorado Springs
719-235-5477, loyalcoffee.co

Brooklyn's on Boulder
110 E. Boulder St., Colorado Springs
719-415-3115, brooklynsonboulder.com

Urban Steam
1025 S. Sierra Madre St., Colorado Springs
719-473-7832, urbansteam.com

Chiba Bar
19 E. Kiowa St., Colorado Springs
719-635-9599, chiba-bar.com

SHAKE HANDS
WITH CELEBRITY CHEFS

Downtown on Tejon Street, two restaurants next door to one another have become Celebrity Chef Central. The two chefs who've taken up shop here, Brother Luck and Mark Henry, have together competed on five Food Network and Bravo cooking shows. Luck scored a win on *Beat Bobby Flay,* and Henry took the top spots on *Cooks vs. Cons* and *Chopped.*

Neither has let the celeb status get to his head though. They just keep chatting up locals and tourists alike, and churning out creative, quality dishes.

At Four by Brother Luck, the seasonally changing menu focuses on dishes from "the hunter, the gatherer, the fisherman, and the farmer." And next door, Rooster's House of Ramen's tagline says it all: "Make America slurp again."

Four by Brother Luck
321 N. Tejon St., Colorado Springs
719-434-2741, fourbybrotherluck.com

Rooster's House of Ramen
323 N. Tejon St., Colorado Springs
719-578-3031, makeamericaslurpagain.com

TIP

Heidi Trelstad, owner of Chef Sugar's Cakes and Confections, has competed in two Food Network competition shows. She lost both, but she's still a big winner in the Springs. Chef Aaron Rivera also beat Bobby Flay when he was living in Charlotte, North Carolina, and earning awards for his previous restaurant, Tapas 51. Brother Luck recruited Rivera to move here in 2017, and since then Rivera opened Canela Coffee and Market.

Chef Sugar's Cakes and Confections
6942 N. Academy Blvd., Colorado Springs
719-260-8600, chefsugar.com

Canela Coffee and Market
2424 Garden of the Gods Rd., Colorado Springs
719-593-1610, canelacoffee.com

20

LINE UP A FLIGHT AT THE WINERY

AT HOLY CROSS ABBEY

Opened in 2002, the Winery at Holy Cross Abbey ranks among the top five largest wineries in the state, producing more than twelve thousand cases each year. Of the fourteen wines currently featured, you can sample ten for free at the Abbey's Tasting Room. (The other four are reserves; a taste of each costs one dollar.)

If you'd prefer to settle in for a bit and enjoy some munchables with your wine, reserve a summertime VIP tasting on the terrace. A cheery and knowledgeable host will introduce you to each pour and advise you which of the options—cheese, bread, fruit, or chocolate—will best complement each wine.

Winery at Holy Cross Abbey
3011 E. Hwy. 50, Cañon City
719-276-5191, abbeywinery.com

21

DROWN YOURSELF IN GREEN CHILI
AT KING'S CHEF

No matter which of two downtown King's Chef Diner locations you choose to stuff your face at, you'll get to order specialty items with names like The Thing, The Grump, and the Merl Scramble. The Food Network-award-winning breakfast burrito is also available at both cash-only diners, as is Colorado green chili. If you don't get your fill of green chili during breakfast or lunch, buy a jar to take home.

What you can get at only one location, however, is the ambiance of an original Valentine diner built in 1955 and opened as King's Chef a year later. The thirteen-seat purple castle on Costilla Street is believed to be one of the only custom designs produced by the manufacturing company.

King's Chef Diner
Original Purple Castle Diner: 110 E. Costilla St., Colorado Springs
719-634-9135
131 E. Bijou St., Colorado Springs
719-636-5010, cosdiner.com

Ent Center for the Arts
(Credit: Kirsten Akens)

ARTS AND ENTERTAINMENT

22

LEARN TO BOOT SCOOT AND TWO-STEP

AT COWBOY'S

When attendees at Cowboy's weekly country line-dance lessons master another eight-count, instructor Barb Thacker typically exclaims, "Sah-weet!" It's a word she's repeated as two syllables and with a bit of a Southern accent hundreds of times over the twenty-plus years she's taught at the popular Western-themed nightclub. It's this enthusiasm coupled with her fun-loving, kind-hearted nature that keep people coming back week after week to learn the latest dance crazes as well as the classics for just five dollars.

But when Thacker's done, the lessons aren't. Manny and Alice Rodela teach traditional couples' dance moves, including two-step, East and West Coast swing, country cha-cha, and waltz—one style a week, on a rotating basis. They're a bit more reserved than Thacker but by no means less experienced as teachers.

Cowboy's
25 N. Tejon St., Colorado Springs
719-596-1212, csnightclubs.com/cowboys

23

GO AWOL
AT THE ENT CENTER FOR THE ARTS

Outdoor public sculpture took a big step forward in Colorado Springs with the 2018 opening of the Ent Center for the Arts at the University of Colorado Colorado Springs (UCCS). As a part of AWOL: Art WithOut Limits, a program of the UCCS Galleries of Contemporary Art, a half-dozen site-specific pieces are on temporary display for six months to two years at a time.

The inaugural season includes three futuristic steel sculptures by world-renowned local artist Starr Kempf: Space Needle, Metronome, and a towering steel rooster titled Sunrise Serenade. Wander the Ent Center grounds and spend some time with these pieces and others before catching a theater, dance, or music performance inside the stunning new visual and performing arts complex.

Ent Center for the Arts at UCCS
5225 N. Nevada Ave., Colorado Springs
719-255-3232, uccs.edu/entcenter

TIP

Though Starr Kempf died in 1995, family members maintain his home in Cheyenne Cañon. Some of the sculptures he erected on the grounds can be seen from the street at 2057 Pine Grove Ave. (Just be respectful of the neighborhood when visiting.)

CHECK OUT ART
ON THE STREETS

Curious about Rusty, the resident concrete, stone, and metal snowman in Acacia Park? The multiple Humpty Dumptys perched precariously on walls about town? Or the purple steel coneflowers forever blooming in the median in front of City Hall? All of these pieces, and about thirty more, are a part of the permanent Art on the Streets collection.

They came out of the more than two-decades-long juried Art on the Streets program, which selects about a dozen new pieces of contemporary sculpture each year for a May debut and one-year display. Pick up an official Downtown Colorado Springs map for a self-guided tour of more than one hundred pieces of city- and privately owned public art on display. And for all the details on how to find each year's new selections, visit the Downtown Partnership's Art on the Streets website.

Art on the Streets
downtowncs.com/aots

TIP

Find free public-art maps at COPPeR (121 S. Tejon St., Suite 111), the Colorado Springs Visitor Center (515 S. Cascade Ave.), or the Downtown Partnership of Colorado Springs (111 S. Tejon St., Suite 703).

25

BE AMAZED BY CIRCUS ACTS AND MORE

AT MILLIBO ART THEATRE

When it comes to stage-based fun, look no further than Millibo Art Theatre, founded by award-winning performer, director, and educator Birgitta De Pree and internationally acclaimed clown Jim Jackson.

It might feel weird to have Jackson, sporting striped pants and a red nose, welcome you into the MAT's former-church home, but it's an indication of the color, creativity, and intimacy that he and De Pree have been serving up since 2001. From the Incredible Circus Millibo and the WTF: Women's Theatre Festival to original plays, hilarious improv, and slinky cabarets, the nonprofit theatre keeps its calendar full, its ticket prices accessible, its unicycles hanging from the ceilings, and its all-ages audience entertained.

Millibo Art Theatre
1626 S. Tejon St., Colorado Springs
719-465-6321, themat.org

26

SING AND DANCE
AT SUMMER MUSIC FESTS

A little over a decade ago, three unrelated groups of musical minds across the community each started up a music-forward festival. Today, all three are bigger and better than ever.

Fiddles, Vittles & Vino, a one-night affair that's put on the last Sunday in June, benefits and is held at Rock Ledge Ranch. It features a nationally touring headliner alongside the food and wine offerings.

Blues Under the Bridge, a full-day event typically held in July under the Colorado Avenue Bridge, brings in a handful of blues performers to help raise funds for Southern Colorado's public radio station 91.5 FM KRCC.

Finally, MeadowGrass is a Memorial Day weekend extravaganza with performances by more than twenty national, regional, and local musicians, food vendors, artist workshops, and optional on-grounds camping at La Foret Conference and Retreat Center supporting the Rocky Mountain Highway Music Collaborative.

Fiddles, Vittles & Vino, fiddlesvittlesandvino.com

Blues Under the Bridge, bluesunderthebridge.org

MeadowGrass, meadowgrass.org

27

SHARE IN THE SHENANIGANS

ON AND OFF THE FIRST FRIDAY SHUTTLE

Jump on the free First Friday Shuttle between five and eight o'clock in the evening to easily hit a multitude of Art Walk destinations in the Creative Corridor of downtown Colorado Springs, Old Colorado City, and Manitou Springs.

Local artists and performers just might be sitting next to you during the ride, ready to bust out a musical interlude or fun facts about Colorado Springs. And though you don't have to get off the shuttle—it can be an evening's worth of entertainment in itself—regular stops include Cottonwood Center for the Arts; the Colorado Springs Fine Arts Center at Colorado College; the downtown arts alley, including The Modbo and S.P.Q.R.; the Art Depot District galleries; and the Manitou Art Center.

First Friday Downtown
downtowncs.com/event/firstfriday

VIEW A FILM
AT KIMBALL'S PEAK THREE

The films, of course, are the main reason to head to Kimball's Peak Three. The only locally owned first-run film theater in Colorado Springs, Kimball's shows mainstream features as well as independent and foreign films on three separate screens—and has been doing so for twenty-five years.

Other reasons to catch a flick here? The intimate downtown location, surrounded by locally owned restaurants of all types, makes for easy dinner-and-a-movie date nights. Then there's the ease of purchasing an adult beverage from the full bar and the enjoyment of drinking it while viewing a film. Adding to the experience is the fresh popcorn, with real butter and free seasonings. And for budget-watchers, the general-admission tickets are the most reasonably priced in the city.

Kimball's Peak Three
115 E. Pikes Peak Ave., Colorado Springs
719-447-1945, kimballspeakthree.com

ASK THE BIG QUESTIONS
AT THE WHAT IF... FESTIVAL

For a full Saturday each September, innovators, creators, and scientists take over six city blocks downtown to offer more than one hundred free interactive experiences for all ages. And the big question of the day is found in this annual festival's name: What IF… Festival of Innovation and Imagination.

What would chalk artists design if they were challenged to paint a block of sidewalk? What could you learn about balance if you tried to walk a slack line a foot above the ground? What could a robot pick up if you programmed her just right? Plan to spend a few hours or the whole day tinkering and challenging your brain, your body, and your soul.

What IF… Festival of Innovation and Imagination
whatif-festival.org

30

SEE ART, MAKE ART, LIVE ART

AT THE FAC

The Colorado Springs Fine Arts Center at Colorado College has exhibited modern American art and brought actors, dancers, and musicians to the stage since it opened in 1936. But its growth into a multidisciplinary museum, theater, and art school—thanks to a building expansion in 2007—has been exponential.

You never know what unique and wonderful experience you'll have. You might find yourself dancing at a silent disco below an art installation of bicycle wheels. You might discover a love of street art at the JAM FAC hip-hop festival.

Of course, it's also perfectly fine to just sit yourself down and have a good think in front of the original John Singer Sargent portrait of Miss Elsie Palmer, the daughter of Colorado Springs founder General William Jackson Palmer. Her portrait is among the many distinguished pieces in the FAC's extensive permanent collection.

Colorado Springs Fine Arts Center at Colorado College
30 W. Dale St., Colorado Springs
719-634-5581, csfineartscenter.org

TIP

The alliance that brought the Colorado Springs Fine Arts Center under the Colorado College umbrella happened in 2017. For visitors, it's meant reduced fees, expanded hours, and a second free museum day each month. But because it also means collaborative initiatives across campus—from visual art exhibitions to high-profile speakers and performers at Edith Kinney Gaylord Cornerstone Arts Center—it's always worth reviewing the college's calendar (coloradocollege.edu/newsevents/calendar) to see what else might be going on.

31

CONNECT WITH PEOPLE ALL OVER THE WORLD

IN THE PORTAL

A few years ago, a large, gold-colored shipping container arrived in Colorado Springs. Inside was the Colorado Springs Portal, which via immersive audiovisual technology transports visitors who step inside to a shared space with a group or an individual somewhere else in the world.

It's a free global public-art project founded by New York-based Shared_Studios that allows one-on-one spatially continuous conversations (with translators as needed). Sponsored by the local nonprofit Imagination Celebration, the Colorado Springs Portal is one of only twenty such containers that are as near as Chicago and as far as Kigali, Rwanda.

The local Portal moves around. You can catch it at a local event or visit the website to find out what location the Springs is currently connecting with, where the Portal is hanging about, and how to sign up for your twenty minutes in what's been aptly described as a life-size Skype box.

Colorado Springs Portal
sharedstudios.com/pikes-peak

ELEVATE VOICES
AT THE ROCKY MOUNTAIN WOMEN'S FILM FESTIVAL

I've spent many a second weekend in November over the past twenty years at the Rocky Mountain Women's Film Festival, watching impactful and thought-provoking films while knee-to-knee with girlfriends in a full theater. RMWFF's history goes back even further, to 1987. The longest continuous-running women's film fest in North America (second internationally to a festival in France), RMWFF today attracts films, directors, producers, and audience members from all over the world.

Of course, despite the honor and the title, know that it's not only women who rack up credits and fill seats. The mission of the fest—and its affiliated nonprofit, the Rocky Mountain Women's Film Institute—is for all people "to elevate the voices of women through film."

Rocky Mountain Women's Film Festival
2727 N. Cascade Ave., Suite 140
719-226-0450, rmwfilminstitute.org

TIP

The annual festival regularly sells out, so plan ahead to attend and order tickets online.

MOVE TO LIVE MUSIC
AT THE BLACK SHEEP

From Imagine Dragons to Dessa and Macklemore to Fitz & the Tantrums, the Black Sheep marquee has featured its share of big names. Recognized as the Best Local Venue for Live Music by the *Colorado Springs Independent* every year since it opened in 2005, the Black Sheep is the spot in Colorado Springs to hear touring musicians and local performers across genres almost every night of the week.

The dark one-room venue caps at 450 standing-room-only concertgoers, which means every show feels intimate and energetic. And when an artist works *Colorado Springs* (or *the Springs*) into a song, the environment kicks up a notch to electric, and power dancers will be glad they left their open-toe shoes at home.

Black Sheep
2106 E. Platte Ave., Colorado Springs
719-227-7625, blacksheeprocks.com

SHIMMY ON OVER
TO A PEAKS AND PASTIES PERFORMANCE

Flying feathers, shimmering sequins, and twirling tassels—oh my! Local burlesque troupe Peaks and Pasties, founded by Lola Spitfire and Ruby Sparkle, celebrated its tenth anniversary in 2018. And it continues to add more cheeky entertainment and skin-baring dancers of all sizes, shapes, and genders.

Catch Bunny Bee, Hazel Humdinger, the Brotherhood of Burlesque, and more, including nationally known touring performers, weekly as a part of The Gold Room's Champagne Cabaret and monthly at the troupe's home stage, Zodiac Venue and Bar—but only if you're twenty-one or older. There's a reason Peaks and Pasties is regularly awarded the local title of Best Naughty Business.

Peaks and Pasties
peaksandpasties.com

35

TAKE IN PROFESSIONAL PRODUCTIONS

AT THE WORLD ARENA AND PIKES PEAK CENTER

When you're craving an evening out to view a super-size production—the likes of Disney on Ice, Cirque du Soleil, or WWE Live—or a super-size star such as Carrie Underwood, Elton John, or Alan Jackson, the eight-thousand-seat Broadmoor World Arena is the local go-to.

The World Arena's sister venue, the two-thousand-seat Pikes Peak Center, is the downtown spot for everything just a little more intimate, a little more cozy, and sometimes a little more local—though no less professional. Think comedians and film fests, touring Broadway musicals and Off-Broadway plays, *The Nutcracker* performed by area dancers, and classical and contemporary concerts by the Colorado Springs Philharmonic.

The Broadmoor World Arena
3185 Venetucci Blvd., Colorado Springs
719-520-SHOW (7649), broadmoorworldarena.com

Pikes Peak Center
190 S. Cascade Ave., Colorado Springs
719-520-SHOW (7649), pikespeakcenter.com

ENGAGE IN INNOVATIVE ARTS
AT GREEN BOX

Green Mountain Falls, population 667, may seem like an odd spot for a dance residency program for New York City's Keigwin + Company. But it has welcomed the contemporary dancers for more than ten years now and also expanded into arguably the most innovative arts festival in the Pikes Peak region.

The heart of the Green Box Arts Festival takes place annually the first week in July and includes more than fifty events, including contemporary art installations such as Tomas Saraceno's Cloud City, concerts, and educational workshops. Dance still plays a key role in the fest. The American Ballet Theatre is one of the more recent companies to perform at the festival, and Colorado Springs-based Ormao Dance Company has collaborated with Larry Keigwin and his dancers to bring original material to the stage.

Green Box Arts Festival, greenboxarts.org

TIP

Each year's full Green Box schedule is typically posted online by May 1. Registration and tickets are available starting June 1.

Labor Day Lift-Off *(Credit: Kirsten Akens)*

SPORTS AND RECREATION

ASCEND
COLORADO SPRINGS' FAMOUS FOURTEENER

The ways to get to the top of Pikes Peak (and back down) are as varied as the activities around the 14,115-foot mountain.

Hike the thirteen-mile one-way, 7,400-foot vertical gain Barr Trail or the much-less-traveled 13.6-mile round-trip Crags route. Drive, bike, or grab a shuttle along the nineteen-mile Pikes Peak Highway. Boat, standup paddle-board, or fish as many as three reservoirs. Snap photos of flora and fauna. Munch a world-famous high-altitude-fried donut at the Summit House. The last Sunday in June, cheer on Pikes Peak International Hill Climb competitors; and in late August, root for your favorite Pikes Peak Ascent and Marathon racers.

However you spend your time on the mountain, bring layers. The temperature at the top of Pikes Peak is typically thirty to forty degrees cooler than at the bottom, and weather conditions can change rapidly.

Pikes Peak
coloradosprings.gov/pikes-peak-americas-mountain?mlid=9051

Since 1891, the Pikes Peak Cog Railway has been one of the most popular routes up and down the mountain. But in 2018, the owners determined that the Cog's equipment and infrastructure needed major repairs and restoration, and they stopped running the iconic train. Hopes are that it will be back on the tracks by 2020.

38

WANDER
GARDEN OF THE GODS

The story of Garden of the Gods begins millions of years ago. So do drop by Garden of the Gods Visitor and Nature Center and wander through the exhibits to learn a bit about the geological, ecological, and historical history. But pick up a free full-color trail map, and get back outside as soon as you can.

What's most important here is experiencing the majestic, three-hundred-foot-tall, red-orange sandstone rocks of this city park that's one of just six hundred National Natural Landmarks in the United States. Get up close while hiking on the fifteen miles of trails—some easy, some moderate—or drive through the park and stop at iconic formations such as Balanced Rock and Kissing Camels.

Garden of the Gods Visitor and Nature Center
1805 N. Thirtieth St., Colorado Springs
719-634-6666, gardenofgods.com

39

HIKE
THE CITY

When it comes to hiking, running, mountain biking, or dog walking in Colorado Springs, some of the best spots are those that are tucked among residential neighborhoods, strip malls, and major thoroughfares but still seem miles from civilization.

Palmer Park boasts twenty-five miles of trails on 730 acres right in the heart of the city. The 538-acre Ute Valley Park, at the northwest end of town, features a 3.5-mile loop, with multiple offshoot and cross trails. The southwest Stratton Open Space, with its 318 acres, has eight miles of trails that pass through five ecosystems. And Pulpit Rock Park, a part of the five-hundred-acre Austin Bluffs Open Space at the northeast end of the city, offers an easy 1.5-mile hike that ends with a challenging scramble to access sweeping city views at the Pulpit Rock summit.

Palmer Park, 3650 Maizeland Rd., Colorado Springs
coloradosprings.gov/parks/page/palmer-park

Ute Valley Park, 1705 Vindicator Dr., Colorado Springs
coloradosprings.gov/parks/page/ute-valley-park

Stratton Open Space, 1504 Ridgeway Ave., Colorado Springs
coloradosprings.gov/parks/page/stratton-open-space

Pulpit Rock Park, 5547 Nevada Frontage Rd., Colorado Springs
coloradosprings.gov/parks/page/austin-bluffs-open-space

STRAP
ON SOME ICE SKATES

The first ice-skating arena to open in Colorado Springs was The Broadmoor Ice Palace in 1938. A year later, the year-round facility became the home for the Pikes Peak Figure Skating Club, which would soon become an official member of the US Figure Skating Association. Arena and club names have changed over the years, but Olympic hopefuls and gold-medal-winning athletes living and training here have continued the legacy of skating.

Today, three facilities offer indoor public-skate sessions: Sertich Ice Center, Honnen Ice Arena, and The Broadmoor World Arena Ice Hall. Perhaps the most fun opportunity to intentionally slip and slide on ice, however, is during the winter holiday season, when Downtown Colorado Springs opens Skate in the Park, a temporary rink in Acacia Park.

Sertich Ice Center at Memorial Park
1705 E. Pikes Peak Ave., Colorado Springs
719-385-5983, coloradosprings.gov/sertich-ice-center/page/public-skating

Honnen Ice Arena at Colorado College
30 W. Cache la Poudre St., Colorado Springs
719-389-6157, coloradocollege.edu/other/honnen/public-skating

The Broadmoor World Arena Ice Hall
3185 Venetucci Blvd., Colorado Springs
719-477-2178, broadmoorworldarena.com/arena-info/icehall

Skate in the Park
downtowncs.com/event/skate-in-the-park

SHRED

MEMORIAL PARK SKATE PARK

At forty thousand square feet, the city-owned Memorial Park Skate Park is the second largest in the state. Built by award-winning design firm Team Pain, the free and open-to-the-public concrete facilities offer everything a shredder could want, including a twenty-thousand-square-foot street course; smooth bowls; a pool with stairs, a love seat, and a death box; six-foot and fourteen-foot vertical ramps; and stadium-style lights allowing late-night runs.

All these bells and whistles have made the skate park the home of the annual Rocky Mountain Rampage, a summertime competition founded by local skateboarders that's given amateurs the chance to break into the pro ranks and spectators the chance to watch some sweet sessions.

Memorial Park Skate Park
1705 E. Pikes Peak Ave., Colorado Springs
visitcos.com/directory/skateboard-park-in-memorial-park-parks-and-open-spaces

42

EXPLORE
PAINT MINES INTERPRETIVE PARK

After driving about forty minutes east from downtown Colorado Springs through El Paso County prairieland, hiking into the massive geological formations of Paint Mines Interpretive Park feels a bit like being transported to another planet or time. As the grasslands slip away, rock spires and hoodoos stand tall, displaying stunning red, pink, orange, and yellow bands of clay caused by oxidized iron compounds.

American Indians have visited the area for hundreds of years to gather the colored clay to produce paint for pottery, but they weren't the first people drawn to this particular space. Prehistoric people inhabited the 750 acres nearly nine thousand years ago. Today, you can openly wander the same ground on which these Paleoindians lived, loved, and hunted deer, caribou, and the now-extinct mammoth.

Paint Mines Interpretive Park
29950 Paint Mines Rd., Calhan
719-520-7529, communityservices.elpasoco.com/parks-and-recreation/paint-mines-interpretive-park/

INDOOR CLIMB AND MORE
AT CITYROCK

With forty-three-foot walls and fifteen thousand square feet of roped climbing, CityROCK Climbing Center is the spot for indoor rock climbers to chalk up their hands and test their skills on slabs, cracks, and overhangs.

But that's not where the downtown facility's activities end. Those more interested in bouldering have 5,000 square feet of surface to traverse. Those not interested in heights of any sort can drop by to spectate during youth and adult competitions, take a yoga or strength-training class, or grab a draft at The Ute & Yeti. Housed at the front of the former theater, the pub and café is a local favorite for its extensive beer list and solid food menu of salads, sandwiches, and flatbreads.

CityROCK Climbing Center
21 N. Nevada Ave., Colorado Springs
719-634-9099, climbcityrock.com

HARNESS UP
FOR OUTDOOR CLIMBING

One of the first technical rock-climbing areas in the United States was established in Garden of the Gods, with many of the routes developed more than a century ago. Climbers and boulderers still traverse the park's sandstone today or tackle other local routes at Red Rock Canyon Open Space, Ute Valley Park, and North Cheyenne Cañon.

For a longer crag session, a ninety-minute drive south drops climbers at the vertical limestone of the Bureau of Land Management's Shelf Road. One of the most popular sport climbing areas statewide, Shelf Road features about one thousand bolted routes among six main climbing venues located between Cañon City and Cripple Creek. All are free, open to the public, and, with moderate temperatures even in winter, climbable year-round.

Bureau of Land Management's Shelf Road
blm.gov/visit/search-details/16855/2

RIDE
THE VELODROME

Whether you're a kid or a kid at heart, stepping through the airlock entry at the Colorado Springs Olympic Training Center Velodrome inspires smiles. There's nothing fancy about it, but how many places in this world are there that bring to life what feels like a moment from a favorite sci-fi film?

Once through the entry, walk a short tunnel and arrive in the center of the 333.3-meter banked cement track. Overhead sits a seven-story-tall, five-basketball-court-long white dome—an upgrade added to the site in 2015 to ensure a year-round, climate-controlled environment for the Olympic athletes who train here. You don't have to be a pro to test it out (or spectate). Along with races and training sessions, USA Cycling coaches and elite athletes offer weekly clinics for those wanting to give it a spin.

Colorado Springs Olympic Training Center Velodrome
250 S. Union Blvd., Colorado Springs
719-352-9475, teamusa.org/velo

VISIT CHEYENNE CAÑON
FOR OUTDOOR ADVENTURE OF ALL SORTS

It's really difficult to pick a favorite adventure in North Cheyenne Cañon Park. The 1,626-acre southwest-side city park brims with potential, whether you're a hiker, a mountain biker, a runner, an equestrian, a rock climber, a plein-air painter, a hummingbird watcher, a wildflower photographer, or just a kid (or a leashed dog) who wants to splash in a cold creek.

Two visitor centers, Starsmore Visitor and Nature Center and Helen Hunt Falls Visitor Center, are staffed throughout the summer by knowledgeable folks who will answer your questions about the area. Have fun in the park, but keep in mind that this is bear and mountain lion country, so it's wise to use extra caution.

North Cheyenne Cañon Park
coloradosprings.gov/page/north-cheyenne-canon

Starsmore Visitor and Nature Center
2120 S. Cheyenne Cañon Rd., Colorado Springs
719-385-6086

Helen Hunt Falls Visitor Center
3440 N. Cheyenne Cañon Rd., Colorado Springs
719-633-5701

47

STEP IT UP
ON THE MANITOU SPRINGS INCLINE

The Incline is no joke: 2,744 steps, just under one mile in length, with a two-thousand-foot elevation gain that tops out at a height of 8,600 feet. The average grade of the former cable-car track is 45 percent (at its steepest, 68 percent).

Yet hikers, runners, and amateur and professional athletes alike not only survive the climb, but make this extreme trail a regular part of their exercise routines. Some complete it in twenty minutes; others take a few hours. All know that no matter how fast they're moving, it's important to be at least somewhat cautious when climbing the railroad-tie staircase.

Thankfully, they don't have to be cautious about one issue anymore. What used to be illegal until 2013 is now a private-public collaboration, free and open to all.

Manitou Springs Incline
The bottom of the Incline is located behind the upper Pikes Peak Cog Railway parking lot, on Ruxton Avenue in Manitou Springs.
inclinefriends.org

TIP

Plan to pay for parking unless you park on the lot behind the former Tajine Alami Moroccan Restaurant at 10 Old Man's Trail and take the free shuttle. It runs every twenty minutes from 6:00 a.m. to 6:00 p.m.

ROLL THOSE MOUNTAINS
ON TWO WHEELS

Colorado Springs is a mountain biker's paradise. More than sixty miles of unpaved mountain-bike trails sit within city limits, and even more are just outside those limits.

Both beginners and those with intermediate skills will enjoy the Air Force Academy's thirteen-mile, mostly single-track Falcon Trail loop with its scenic views. Those with more experience will want to test their mettle on Captain Jack's Trail, named for Captain Ellen Jack, a prospector and gold miner who opened a Wild West-themed cabin resort near the trailhead in the early 1900s. She likely would approve of mountain-biking thrill seekers who plan their routes to hit her namesake trail as a downhill so they can push their speeds.

Falcon Trail
usafa.edu/visitors/hiking-biking-trails

Captain Jack's Trail
cheyennecanon.org/captain-jacks

TIP

For regional trail maps and updated trail conditions, visit Medicine Wheel Trail Advocates, the local International Mountain Bicycling Association chapter, at medwheel.org.

GET MOVIN'
AT RED ROCK CANYON OPEN SPACE

Nearly 1,500 acres of open space. Miles of trails open to hikers, runners, bikers, and equestrians. Two off-leash loops for happy pups. Eighty-five rock-climbing routes. A free-ride bike park. A paragliding launch. A couple picnic areas.

There's a lot going on at Red Rock Canyon Open Space, which is why one of the premier spots to sneak away to is the hikers-only Contemplative Trail. Built by the Garden of the Goddesses Club, the meditative 1.75-mile trail on the west side of the park features towering rock walls for shade, pine benches for pausing, and oodles and oodles of quiet.

Red Rock Canyon Open Space
redrockcanyonopenspace.org

CONQUER THE UNDERGROUND
AT CAVESIM

If crawling around in dark, tight spaces makes you panicky, you might want to skip CaveSim. But if the idea of exploring 225 feet of artificial cave passages gives you the good kind of goose bumps, keep reading.

CaveSim, housed at CityRock Climbing Gym, is the only permanent electronic cave simulator in the world, created by Manitou Springs residents Dave and Tracy Jackson. The two travel the country with a sixty-foot mobile sim unit, training search-and-rescue personnel and teaching cave conservation.

But at CaveSim, you'll don a helmet, a headlamp, and kneepads, and shimmy through three-foot-tall by 2.5-foot-wide passages and around electronically sensored stalactites, stalagmites, and other formations. How carefully you go is tracked on a computer, so every time you come, you can try to improve your skills.

CaveSim
21 N. Nevada Ave., Colorado Springs
719-634-9099, cavesim.com

51

CLIMB THE STAIRS
AT SEVEN FALLS

Climbing the 224 steps alongside The Broadmoor's Seven Falls is not a requirement for getting to the top or back down—there's a mountain elevator for those who need it—but it's an exhilarating way to experience what's known as The Grandest Mile of Scenery in Colorado. As the falls cut through the 790-foot-tall pink granite of the Pillars of Hercules, they send 181 feet of water cascading down this natural box canyon.

Other activities at the falls include two hiking trails, the Seven Falls souvenir shop, Rockhounds at the Eagle's Nest, and Restaurant 1858. The newest addition is The Broadmoor's separately ticketed Soaring Adventure at Seven Falls, which includes ten zip lines divided between two courses and other aerial activities high above the canyon.

Seven Falls
Parking is located at 1045 Lower Gold Camp Road.

Soaring Adventures
Parking is in The Broadmoor's East Lot at 6 Lake Avenue.
broadmoor.com/broadmoor-adventures/seven-falls

FISH, TUBE, AND SAIL

LAKE PUEBLO

With large bodies of water in short supply within the Springs' city limits, a great escape when the Colorado sun pounds down is Lake Pueblo's sixty miles of shoreline and 4,600 surface acres of water just a fifty-minute drive south. Water recreation here includes kayaking, river tubing, sailing, waterskiing, motor boating, and fishing. If you want to mix some dry with the wet, surrounding the lake are almost ten thousand acres with trails for hiking and biking.

Play for a half or full day (a daily pass costs seven dollars) or stay overnight at one of four hundred campsites ($18-$24 per night). If you get an itch for caffeine, run into town to Solar Roast Coffee, and while you're in the area, pop over to the mile-long Pueblo Riverwalk for an infusion of art and history.

Lake Pueblo State Park
640 Pueblo Reservoir Rd., Pueblo
cpw.state.co.us/placestogo/parks/LakePueblo

Solar Roast Coffee
226 N. Main St., Pueblo
719-544-2008, solarroast.com

Pueblo Riverwalk
puebloriverwalk.org

53

GOLF BETTER THAN PAR
AT PATTY JEWETT

The views of Pikes Peak can be distracting from the city-owned Patty Jewett Golf Course, but try to keep your eyes on the ball or you might lose it in one of the old, but not as old as the course, century-tall trees. Built in 1898, downtown's Patty Jewett is the third-oldest public course west of the Mississippi. Local businessman William Jewett purchased the property in 1910 and deeded it to the city in 1919 with the understanding that it would honor his wife, who had died four years earlier.

After viewing Patty's portrait in the clubhouse, walk or grab a cart for the par seventy-two, eighteen-hole course. Or jump on the nine-hole course and enjoy this local favorite for players of any skill level.

Patty Jewett Golf Course
900 E. Espanola St., Colorado Springs
719-385-6950, coloradosprings.gov/patty-jewett-golf-course

54

PEEP
THE CHANGING ASPEN LEAVES

Ever heard of *leaf peeping*? It's a very Colorado activity of seeking out aspen-tree-heavy areas by foot or car to soak up (and Instagram) the vibrant reds, yellows, and oranges that paint the leaves each fall. Peak season, when the most foliage is sporting brilliant colors, generally occurs between mid-September and mid-October, but both weather and elevation affect the dates.

Two spots near the Springs worth checking out are Mueller State Park for those wanting to hike and Highway 67 through Cripple Creek for those preferring a drive. Getting to both places means passing through Woodland Park, so plan a stop at The Donut Mill, the bakery that's been pleasing locals and tourists alike every bit as much as quaking aspen leaves have for more than thirty-five years.

Mueller State Park
21045 Hwy. 67 South, Divide
719-687-2366, cpw.state.co.us/placestogo/parks/Mueller

Cripple Creek
visitcripplecreek.com

The Donut Mill
310 E. Midland Ave., Woodland Park
719-687-9793, thedonutmill.com

SLED, STARGAZE, AND SIT SILENTLY
AT THE GREAT SAND DUNES

Visitors to Great Sand Dunes National Park and Preserve can do all the expected things: hike, backpack, camp, picnic, watch wildlife, and splash in creek waters. But there are three not-so-typical activities that everyone should do within the thirty-square-mile dune field.

First, sled or sand-board. Bring your own gear or rent locally. Hike up to tackle the first high ridge of dunes. Scream and smile all the way down; then turn around, hike back up, and give it another go.

Second, visit after dark because the park is open 24/7. Hike without flashlights under a full moon, or see the stars like you've never seen them on moonless nights.

Finally, simply sit and take in the tallest dunes in North America. Feel soft sand in your toes. Watch cloud shadows drift. Connect with the eleven-thousand-year history that humans have with this majestic place.

Great Sand Dunes National Park and Preserve
Visitor Center, 11999 State Hwy. 150, Mosca
719-378-6395, nps.gov/grsa/index.htm

GAPE AT 250,000 BATS
AT ORIENT LAND TRUST

Bats are a big deal at the 2,200-acre protected open space in the northern San Luis Valley known as Orient Land Trust. In addition to ten small colonies that live on the property year-round, the largest migratory colony of Mexican free-tailed bats in Colorado has roosted here every summer for more than fifty years.

Other states can claim larger numbers—the Austin, Texas, colony, for example, tops 1.5 million bats, six times as many as OLT. But OLT's colony is unique because it's majority male.

After checking in at the Welcome Center, visitors can hike the two miles to the Orient Mine on their own to see the massive bat outflight or participate in a free guided summer evening hike that leaves from the center a few hours before dusk.

Orient Land Trust
64393 County Rd. GG, Moffat
719-256-4315, olt.org

TIP

The drive from Colorado Springs is about three hours, so go for the bats and the hiking, and stay for the soaking and lodging at Valley View Hot Springs. If you forget your swimsuit, no worries. As one of the few naturist properties in the state, clothing is optional in Orient Land Trust.

SOAK
AT SUNWATER SPA

Relaxing in one of eight cedar tubs filled with solar-panel-heated, mineral-laden Seven Minute Spring water at SunWater Spa is a delight any time of day. Relaxing in the tubs after dusk, when stars begin to twinkle above Red Mountain, is dreamy.

But don't let all that relaxation keep you from walking the river-rock-bottomed meditation stream, finding a hammock or swing chair to lounge in, or catching your breath under the cold plunge pool's bamboo shower. You can also take a yoga class, experience an individual or couples massage, float through a Watsu body therapy session in the saline pool, or schedule an overnight stay at partner SunMountain Center. (Of course, we won't judge you if you seek out one tub and stay in it your entire visit.)

SunWater Spa
514 El Paso Blvd., Manitou Springs
719-695-7007, sunwellness.net

UNVEIL THE MAGIC OF HOT-AIR BALLOONS

ON LABOR DAY

One of the best ways to experience the more than forty-year tradition that is the Labor Day Lift-Off is to be in Memorial Park at seven o'clock in the morning, Saturday through Monday of Labor Day weekend, surrounded by some seventy hot-air balloons waiting to take off. If you're near Prospect Lake, you can even catch some of the balloons dipping down to skim the waters before heading up and away.

That's not the only way to experience the magic though. Purchase a ride on one of the balloons or volunteer to crew. Or at dusk Saturday and Sunday, attend the annual Balloon Glow. There, crews will set up, inflate their balloons, and ignite their burners, lighting up the night skies to the sound of cheers all around.

Labor Day Lift-Off
Memorial Park, 1705 E. Pikes Peak Ave., Colorado Springs
coloradospringslabordayliftoff.com

HUG ZIGGY
AT A SWITCHBACKS FOOTBALL MATCH

Every professional sports team needs a winning mascot. And the United Soccer League recently named Colorado Springs Switchbacks Football Club's Ziggy the Mountain Goat as one of the Top 5 in the league. He's a friendly guy who wanders Weidner Field during matches, happily giving out hugs, posing with a big grin, and photo-bombing selfies. He's even received a fashion makeover since the Switchbacks' opening game in 2015, changing out lederhosen for his very own black and royal blue striped team uniform.

Ziggy's not the only team member fans can connect with at the fifteen-plus home games a year. After matches, players head for the stands to sign autographs and smile through their sweat for photos. It's that kind of sport.

Switchbacks Football Club
Weidner Field, 6303 Barnes Rd., Colorado Springs
719-368-8480, switchbacksfc.com

60

GEAR UP
FOR A BASEBALL DOUBLE SWITCH

Baseball in Colorado Springs has big changes ahead. After thirty years here, in 2019 the Triple-A Minor League Sky Sox will be transferred to Texas to continue on as the San Antonio Missions. The Sky Sox stadium, Security Service Field, will become the home of the rookie-league Helena Brewers of the Pioneer League, under new branding as the Rocky Mountain Vibes.

The team will still feed into the Milwaukee Brewers, although the season will be shorter and eliminate the impact of springtime low temps and snow. But several fan faves will remain. The 8,500-capacity stadium will reportedly still offer fireworks, along with discount days and other special promotions that fans have come to love. And no matter the hitters or the team brand, the balls will still fly at the highest-altitude professional baseball stadium in the United States.

Baseball at Security Service Field
4385 Tutt Blvd., Colorado Springs
milb.com/colorado-springs

GET STARRY-EYED
WITH THE ASTRONOMICAL SOCIETY

On a clear night in the Pikes Peak region, it's easy to head outside, look up to the skies, and stare at the moon and the stars. If you want to take your night-sky-staring up a notch though, the Colorado Springs Astronomical Society offers a multitude of public events, from full-moon astronomy hikes at Garden of the Gods to star parties at dark-sky locations across the region with members and their telescopes on hand.

The society's biggest event of each year, however, is the all-ages summertime Rocky Mountain Star Stare. For more than thirty years, the thirty-five-acre Starry Meadows, just outside Gardner, Colorado, has welcomed hundreds of amateurs and professionals alike to spend four days camping and solar observing from a property where darkness levels get as deep as 21.95 on a twenty-two-point scale—in laymen's terms, really, really, really dark.

Colorado Springs Astronomical Society
csastro.org

BIKE DOWNTOWN
WITH PIKERIDE

Downtown Colorado Springs is pretty walkable, but for adults eighteen and older who want to get around a little wider distance in the city center a little faster, there's PikeRide. Launched in 2018 by Downtown Ventures, the twelve-square-mile bike-share system currently includes 206 eight-speed bicycles, twenty-eight hubs, and six solar-powered payment kiosks. Just two dollars will get a rider thirty minutes with a bike, and more time can be added as needed.

Grab a PikeRide and cycle to lunch, do some shopping, and visit a downtown museum. Or pedal out to Pikes Peak Greenway Trail for a leisurely ride along Monument Creek, south to America the Beautiful Park or north (and a few blocks east) to Lincoln Center.

PikeRide
pikeride.org

63

GRAB YOUR TIGER TAIL

FOR A CC TIGER HOCKEY MATCH

Colorado College Tiger Hockey debuted in January 1938 with a first-game 8-1 loss to a team sponsored by the now-defunct Giddings Department Store. Since then, the team has improved quite a bit. Two national championships. Twenty NCAA tournament appearances. Nine conference titles. Two Hobey Baker Memorial Award winners. Thirty-two National Hockey League players. Forty-five All-Americans. Eleven consecutive winning seasons. And a seasoned head coach, Mike Haviland, who led the Chicago Blackhawks to the Stanley Cup in 2010.

Grab your Tiger tail, join the more than six thousand other fans at a home ice match, and cheer on one of the top college sports teams in the region.

Tiger Hockey at The Broadmoor World Arena (October through March)
3185 Venetucci Blvd., Colorado Springs
719-389-6342, cctigers.com

64

CHEER ON
AIR FORCE FOOTBALL

Football games at the Air Force Academy's Falcon Stadium are as much about the production around the game as the match-up itself. For starters, expect a lot of noise, from the cheering of an audience of forty thousand, to the Drum and Bugle Corps' entertainment, to the flyovers one minute before kickoff.

And take time to appreciate the precision of the cadet squadrons as they march onto the field to salute the flag during the national anthem. You'll see them again after the kickoff, during freshman push-ups at the end zone each time the Falcons score a touchdown. As for halftime, it's a show in itself, with the Wings of Blue sky-dive team and prairie falcon demonstrations regular fare.

No doubt about it. The Blue and Grey like to put on a winning show, on field and off.

Air Force Football at Falcon Stadium
2169 Field House Dr., US Air Force Academy
719-472-1895, goairforcefalcons.com, aftickets.com

65

RETREAT
AT THE BENEDICTINE SPIRITUALITY CENTER IN THE PINES

The labyrinth at Benedictine Spirituality Center in the Pines is one of ten designated spots for meditation and contemplation on the forty-four-acre property. It's one of the most natural as well, built into the forest ground and around Ponderosa pine.

Walk the path, then wander to a few of the other meditation spaces. From Zen gardens and a stone grotto to the fourteen Stations of the Cross, each place offers different focus and perspective for those of all (or no) faith traditions.

The Sisters of Benet Hill Monastery, who run and live on the property, welcome guests for an hour, a day, a meal and prayers, an overnight hermitage stay, or an extended retreat. (Fees vary for these retreat options.) The Sisters ask that guests for a short drop-by visit check in at the information desk.

Benedictine Spirituality Center in the Pines
3190 Benet Ln., Colorado Springs
719-633-0655, benethillmonastery.org

Benet Hill Monastery
(Credit: Kirsten Akens)

Colorado Springs Pioneers Museum
(Credit: Kirsten Akens)

CULTURE AND HISTORY

66

TOUR
THE AIR FORCE ACADEMY CAMPUS

The icon of the United States Air Force Academy is Cadet Chapel. According to the academy, the 150-foot glass, steel, and aluminum structure is the most popular man-made attraction in Colorado, with more than half a million visitors each year.

Unfortunately, the chapel's seventeen soaring spires are leaking, and the National Historic Landmark will be closed in 2019 for up to four years of renovation. That's a bummer, but many other spots at the academy are worth a stop: the thirty-five-thousand-square-foot Visitors Center; the Honor Court (especially when the cadet wing marches in formation to lunch); the Field House, Falcon Stadium, and Athletic Center; and Stanley Canyon and Falcon trails. Add to the list anywhere you can look up and see cadets flying gliders.

US Air Force Academy Visitors Center
2346 Academy Dr., US Air Force Academy
719-333-2025, usafa.edu/academics/facilities/visitors-center/

TIP

The newly renovated planetarium, which has been closed since 2004, is scheduled to open in 2019. So you might miss seeing the chapel, but you could be among the first to visit one of the oldest buildings on campus and its highly anticipated new digital dome.

IMMERSE IN LOCAL HISTORY

AT PIONEERS MUSEUM

Whatever Pikes Peak region-related history and culture is on display from the Colorado Springs Pioneers Museum's impressive sixty-thousand-object collection is always worth seeing, as is the museum's handful of permanent exhibits. But the draw for many who visit this free municipal museum is the downtown facility itself, the fully restored 1903 El Paso County courthouse.

Ride the 1913 Otis cast-iron birdcage elevator to the third floor. Sit in a gallery chair in the restored Division I Courtroom. View murals by one of America's most renowned mural painters, local artist Eric Bransby, and imagine the area from the time the first humans lived on these lands through the 1960s.

Colorado Springs Pioneers Museum
215 S. Tejon St., Colorado Springs
719-385-5990, cspm.org

BE A VIP
AT THE OLYMPIC TRAINING CENTER

During a recent VIP tour at the US Olympic Training Center, I got schooled in pentathlon by High Performance Director Dr. Genadijus Sokolovas. For the rest of my life, I'll be able to recite that modern pentathlon includes five disciplines inspired by the ancient Olympics: fencing, swimming, equestrian show jumping, pistol shooting, and cross-country running.

The standard hour-long public tour (for fifteen dollars) includes all sorts of cool experiences: seeing the climate-control room for acclimatizing athletes, observing the "antigravity" treadmills, and popping in on a wheelchair-basketball match. But if you've got a passion for the Olympic and Paralympic Games, splurge on the behind-the-scenes version. For seventy-five dollars per person, you'll get three hours with a guide and lunch in the athlete cafeteria, where you just might see your favorite US Olympian.

US Olympic Training Center
1 Olympic Plaza, Colorado Springs
719-866-4618, teamusa.org/about-the-usoc/olympic-training-centers/csotc/tours

A brand-new, sixty-thousand-square-foot United States Olympic Museum is scheduled to open in 2019, featuring the US Olympic Hall of Fame, twenty thousand square feet of highly interactive exhibit space, a state-of-the-art theater, and a gift shop, café, and broadcast studio. Follow its progress and prepare to visit at usolympicmuseum.org.

MEET THE ANIMALS
AT CHEYENNE MOUNTAIN ZOO

Feeding the giraffes at Cheyenne Mountain Zoo can be a slobbery experience. But it's a unique thrill to watch these gentle creatures saunter up, nudge their necks over the fence, stick out their tongues, and grab lettuce-leaf offerings. Put it, and visiting their African Rift Valley home, first on your list of must-do's, and perhaps again at the end.

In between, you've got 146 acres of America's only mountain zoo to wander. Be sure to save time for Rocky Mountain Wild, showcasing the animals that naturally call this area home: moose, porcupines, mountain lions, grizzly bears, North American river otters, Mexican grey wolves, and bald eagles.

Cheyenne Mountain Zoo
4250 Cheyenne Mountain Zoo Rd., Colorado Springs
719-633-9925, cmzoo.org

TIP

The admission fee includes a ticket to visit the Will Rogers Shrine of the Sun. Built by Broadmoor Hotel and Cheyenne Mountain Zoo founder Spencer Penrose, the shrine honors the American humorist and cowboy who was a close friend of Penrose. The shrine is filled with historical mementos and art, and the 1.4-mile drive along Russell Tutt Scenic Highway offers breathtaking views of the city.

DIG INTO
CAVE OF THE WINDS

South Park fans will recognize Cave of the Winds from the "ManBearPig" episode where former Vice President Al Gore takes the kids hunting underground for the elusive creature—and ends up causing "Cave-In of the Winds."

You won't run into any ManBearPigs (or cave-ins) on the forty-five-minute Discovery Tour, but you will get to experience the underground Williams Canyon cave system as a part of a tour history that goes back to 1881. Above ground, the adventures continue with a challenging three-story obstacle course; a virtual-reality theater; a zip line; and the Terror-dactyl, a ride that free-fall drops riders 150 feet down into Williams Canyon.

Cave of the Winds Mountain Park
100 Cave of the Winds Rd., Manitou Springs
719-685-5444, caveofthewinds.com

TIP

The newest addition to Cave of the Winds Mountain Park is a part-hiking, part-climbing, two-hour Via Ferrata tour, one of only four in the state. Designed like the European systems from which it gets its name, this guided canyon tour allows inexperienced climbers to clip on to a track cable and explore the vertical walls sixty feet above the floor of Williams Canyon.

EXPERIENCE THOUSANDS OF BUGS—
WITH NO ITCHING

The world's largest privately owned insect collection resides here in Colorado Springs at May Natural History Museum (often referred to by locals as simply "The Bug Museum"). Beetles, spiders, scorpions, butterflies, moths, and more—seven thousand of them, perfectly preserved, tagged, and pinned—fill the displays that wind through an otherwise no-nonsense roadside attraction that opened in 1952.

To find the entrance, look for the giant Hercules beetle sculpture that sits above Highway 115, and prepare to see some of the most colorful, exotic, and creepy cool creatures ever in one space. All were collected by the museum's namesake, James May; were first displayed by James's son John; and now are being carried on into the future by John's grandson and the current museum president, R.J. Steer, along with other family members.

May Natural History Museum
710 Rock Creek Canyon Rd., Colorado Springs
719-576-0450, coloradospringsbugmuseum.com

May Natural History Museum
(Courtesy Pikes Peak Country Attractions)

SIP
FROM THE MANITOU SPRINGS MINERAL SPRINGS

The mineral springs of Manitou are intricately tied to the history of the town. The Ute Indians in the 1700s believed the bubbly waters to be both the breath of and a gift from the Great Spirit Manitou. Dr. Edwin James, a botanist with the Long Expedition of 1820, was the first Westerner to discover the healing waters rising from cavernous aquifers deep underground. Forty-eight years later, General William Jackson Palmer and Dr. William A. Bell visited the area and saw immense potential for a health resort. In 1871, Manitou Springs was born.

The first to arrive were those suffering from tuberculosis, but by the 1890s, the waters also attracted celebrities and presidents. Today, the Mineral Springs Foundation protects and cares for eight artesian springs whose varying mineral content includes calcium, magnesium, lithium, and zinc. Make the rounds, taste all eight, and find your favorite.

Manitou Springs Mineral Springs
manitoumineralsprings.org

TIP

Visit the Manitou Springs Chamber of Commerce & Visitors Bureau for a free map of the springs, a chart detailing the mineral content of each spring's water, and a sampling cup.

73

PASS SOME TIME
AT THE BROADMOOR

Simple pleasures can be found in abundance on The Broadmoor property. Watch splashing ducks while walking the path around the lake at the resort's center. Enjoy a seasonal, handcrafted cocktail inside at the Summit Lounge or outside by the glow of The Hotel Bar's stone fireplace. View original art in each of the main buildings, including three Maxfield Parrish paintings hanging in the main mezzanine by the fountain.

Of course, more luxurious and adventurous pleasures can also be found in abundance. As the longest-running consecutive winner of both the AAA Five-Diamond and the Forbes Five-Star awards, The Broadmoor has been providing its guests with plush accommodations, PGA and USGA tournament-hosting golf courses, upscale dining, and one of the country's first full-service spas since 1918.

The Broadmoor
1 Lake Ave., Colorado Springs
719-634-7711, broadmoor.com

BUCKLE UP

FOR PIKES PEAK OR BUST RODEO TIME

Rodeo is a rough sport, and rodeo cowboys live a challenging life, traveling the country to keep up with a busy competition schedule. Top talent make competing at the Pikes Peak or Bust Rodeo a priority, not only because it's one of just 650-some Professional Rodeo Cowboys Association-sanctioned rodeos, but also because the PRCA is headquartered here (as is the ProRodeo Hall of Fame).

Featured events during four days of this nearly century-old competition include bareback, saddle bronc, and bull riding; steer wrestling and barrel racing; and team and tie-down roping. And then there's the mutton-bustin', where athletes ages four to nine try to ride a lamb for eight seconds.

Pikes Peak or Bust Rodeo
Norris-Penrose Event Center, 1045 Lower Gold Camp Rd.,
Colorado Springs
719-635-1101, pikespeakorbust.org

ProRodeo Hall of Fame and Museum of the American Cowboy
101 Pro Rodeo Dr., Colorado Springs
719-528-4764, prorodeohalloffame.com

75

CHOOSE
YOUR OWN MUSEUM ADVENTURE

If you or your kids have a particular passion, there's a good chance the Pikes Peak region has a museum for it. Choose your favorite—coins, moon craters, and more—for a few hours of fun and education.

At the American Numismatic Association Money Museum, you'll learn about the art, history, and science of money. The Rocky Mountain Dinosaur Resource Center displays fossil skeletons and life-restoration sculptures alongside a working paleontology laboratory. At the Space Foundation Discovery Center, you'll explore stars, planets, astronauts, space food, and more. And the Western Museum of Mining and Industry digs into everything mining, from gold panning to the impact of the Industrial Revolution.

American Numismatic Association Money Museum
818 N. Cascade Ave., Colorado Springs
800-367-9723, money.org/money-museum

Rocky Mountain Dinosaur Resource Center
201 S. Fairview St., Woodland Park
719-686-1820, rmdrc.com

Space Foundation Discovery Center
4425 Arrowswest Dr., Colorado Springs
719-576-8000, discoverspace.org

Western Museum of Mining and Industry
225 North Gate Blvd., Colorado Springs
719-488-0880, wmmi.org

LIVE THE HISTORY
AT ROCK LEDGE RANCH

While touring Rock Ledge Ranch during its Living History Program, which runs every year from June through August, the common greeting is, "Good day!" It's a nod to life in the Pikes Peak region in the eighteenth and nineteenth centuries, the primary focus of this educational living history farm and museum.

Of course, the American Indians made the Front Range their home for thousands of years earlier, and your first stop on the property will be the late-1700s presettlement American Indian area. As you continue on chronologically, you'll head to the Galloway Homestead (1867–1874), a reconstructed cabin representing prerailroad frontier life.

You'll find original structures as well. Rock Ledge House on Chambers Ranch (1874–1900) and Orchard House (1907–1910) at one time were both owned by Colorado Springs' founder General William Jackson Palmer.

Rock Ledge Ranch
3105 Gateway Rd., Colorado Springs
719-578-6777, rockledgeranch.com

Rock Ledge Ranch hosts about a dozen special events each year, including a Family Fourth celebration, Vintage Labor Day Baseball Game, Garden of the Gods Pow Wow, and fall Harvest Festival. Check the website for these and other opportunities to visit the property in the fall, winter, and spring.

BLAST INTO THE PAST
AT THE MANITOU SPRINGS PENNY ARCADE

From Skeeball lanes and pinball machines to 1980s video games like Ms. Pac-Man and Frogger, the Manitou Springs Penny Arcade in the heart of downtown is filled with more than four hundred options for old-school fun.

Lots of the choices offer a chance to challenge friends or family members to some sort of one-on-one dual. If you're interested in besting a group, up to twelve people can compete in the horse race room—for just fifty cents a person.

Before you head out, fill your pockets with a mix of coins, or plan to slide dollar bills through the change machine. Most play takes quarters, but some of the antique games in the penny arcade room—dating back to the 1930s—do indeed require pennies (and nickels and dimes).

Manitou Springs Penny Arcade, 900 Manitou Ave., Manitou Springs
719-685-9815, facebook.com/manitouspringspennyarcade

TIP

More old-school fun can be found for the young ones in your family at The North Pole—Home of Santa's Workshop (northpolecolorado.com). A Christmas-themed amusement park with rides and shows designed with small children in mind, The North Pole has been a staple in the area since it opened in 1956.

PAUSE FOR A PHOTO
AT THE MESA OVERLOOK

Sometimes, the small parking lot at the Mesa Overlook is filled with chatty, wide-eyed tourists; thirsty, hungry cyclists stopping for water and a snack; and busy families in matching jeans and button-ups shooting photos for their annual holiday cards. Other times, the lot is empty and quiet, and the view of Pikes Peak looming above the Garden of the Gods' towering red-orange sandstone rock formations is magical and holy.

Of course, you can't predict the ambiance you'll encounter on a visit to this easy-to-reach, open-to-the-public spot, just a mile northeast from Garden of the Gods Visitor and Nature Center. Regardless, do take lots of pics. Pretty much any west-facing photo taken sunrise to sunset any day of the year will bring back happy memories and impress friends and family.

Mesa Overlook
3586-3604 Mesa Rd., Colorado Springs

TIP

From Garden of the Gods Visitor and Nature Center, head north on North Thirtieth Street, make a hairpin right turn at Mesa Road, and head back south to the Mesa Overlook parking lot on the right.

FLY HIGH
AT THE NATIONAL MUSEUM OF WORLD WAR II AVIATION

The North American B-25 Mitchell bomber used in the film *Pearl Harbor*, starring Ben Affleck and Josh Harnett, is just one of twenty-some fully restored and operational aircraft in the collection at the National Museum of World War II Aviation. More than one hundred thousand square feet of exhibit space sits on twenty acres adjacent to the Colorado Springs Municipal Airport, more than enough room to also feature thousands of artifacts; historical documents; and an interactive N3N flight simulator, a project of engineering students at the University of Colorado Colorado Springs.

Self-guided tours are always an option. But consider the docent-led tour for the chance to visit WestPac Restorations and watch professionals as they rebuild, repair, and maintain these historical aircraft.

National Museum of World War II Aviation
755 Aviation Way, Colorado Springs
719-637-7559, worldwariiaviation.org

80

RACE COFFINS
AND TOAST EMMA CRAWFORD

In 1889, Emma Crawford arrived in Manitou Springs from Massachusetts, as many did, searching for a cure for her tuberculosis. Before her death in 1891, she asked to be buried on top of nearby Red Mountain. With supportive townspeople, her fiancé carried her coffin up and laid her to rest near the summit.

Unfortunately, the rest was short-lived. Thirty-eight years of snowy winters and heavy spring rains later, Emma and her coffin came rushing back down the mountain. Almost seventy decades later, in 1995, Manitou residents did what only Manitou residents could: they turned her story into macabre entertainment.

Today, nearly ten thousand people flood Manitou every October to attend wakes for Emma at Miramont Castle, cheer on seventy-some fully costumed coffin racers as they race the streets of Manitou two teams at a time, and raise a toast to the town's most famous ghost.

Emma Crawford Coffin Races and Festival
emmacrawfordfestival.com

CELEBRATE THE SEASON
AT THE GLEN EYRIE MADRIGAL BANQUETS

On any average day, Glen Eyrie Castle & Conference Center is a stunning and unexpected sight tucked in the southern end of Queen's Canyon, northeast of Garden of the Gods. But come every December, the Madrigal Banquets turn the English Tudor–style stone building built by Colorado Springs founder General William Jackson Palmer into something magical.

For more than twenty-five years, the castle's Great Hall has become the home for a series of sixteenth-century-inspired, Christmas-celebrating evenings. Costumed performers sing, dance, and otherwise honor and celebrate the season (sometimes in a cheeky fashion) while guests enjoy a four-course meal of tasty dishes, including boar's head as the entrée and The Sweet to finish off the meal.

Glen Eyrie Castle & Conference Center
3820 N. Thirtieth St., Colorado Springs
800-944-4536, gleneyrie.org

TIP

The rest of the year, there's no shortage of things to do at Glen Eyrie, which is a ministry of The Navigators. Enjoy lunch at the coffee shop. Wander shelves of Christian titles in the bookstore. Take a tour and explore the historical and geological wonders of the property. Have a spot of tea. Stay the night for a mini-retreat or a romantic getaway. Room options range from the historic rooms in the castle and the Pink House to classic standard rooms in the lodges.

82

SADDLE UP
FOR WESTERN JUBILEE

The Western Jubilee Warehouse is one of those true hidden gems—in this case, with the shimmer of white cowboy hats and corrugated tin. Tucked away in the historic Santa Fe Rail Yard District, this former freight house holds an intimate theater that's been doing double-duty as a recording studio since the mid-1990s.

The types of albums that come out of Western Jubilee generally fall in the "Western music and cowboy poetry" realm, though owner and proprietor Scott O'Malley has worked more recently with local indie bluegrass band Grass It Up and Pueblo's Americana foursome The Haunted Windchimes.

Billed as both secret and private, concerts here pretty much always sell out. The best way to learn who's coming and when is to sign up for the every-now-and-again newsletter via the website or visit during a public First Friday event.

Western Jubilee Warehouse
433 E. Cucharras St., Colorado Springs
719-635-7776, somagency.com/western-jubilee-warehouse

DISCOVER FOSSILS
IN FLORISSANT

Established in 1969, Florissant Fossil Beds National Monument has been a site for scientific research since the 1870s, and excavations for fossils continue today. You won't find dinosaur fossils, but you will see massive petrified redwood tree stumps while hiking the grounds and tiny fossils from plants, spiders, insects, fish, and seeds—and even fish vomit (the kids will love that!)—in the visitor center.

Just outside the center, a yurt houses the Fossil Learning Lab. The park ranger on duty will help you use microscopes and magnifying glasses to discover new fossils in shale from the area. The rangers are all about teaching visitors, so don't hesitate to ask lots of questions if you have them.

Florissant Fossil Beds National Monument
15807 Teller County Rd. 1, Florissant
719-748-3253, nps.gov/flfo/index.htm

CLAMBER UP

BISHOP CASTLE

Admittedly, the climb up Bishop Castle looks a bit sketchy. And yet, after you've driven ninety minutes south from Colorado Springs and parked along State Highway 165 behind an unbelievably long row of cars, there's an otherworldly draw to the roadside attraction that makes you want to head straight for the stairs and start hoofing it up as high as you can go.

Perhaps the draw comes from knowing that owner Jim Bishop has been constructing the castle by hand, all on his own, for more than sixty years and opens it up for free to the public to visit (donations are welcomed). Perhaps it comes from a desire to try to touch the metal dragon that presides over the property three stories up. Or perhaps there are just some days for throwing logic to the wind, and this is one of them.

Bishop Castle, 12705 State Hwy. 165, Rye
719-564-4366, bishopcastle.org

TIP

From Colorado Springs, the drive south to Bishop Castle takes about ninety minutes on Highway 115 through Florence and along the Frontier Pathways Scenic Byway. Stop about halfway at Coyote's Coffee Den (Highway 115 and Sixth Street) in Penrose for a breakfast burrito and a latté (or a panini for lunch on your return trip to the Springs).

STAND ABOVE
THE ROYAL GORGE

In 2013, a wildfire destroyed 90 percent of the 360-acre Royal Gorge Park in Cañon City, along with most of the buildings and attractions. Thankfully, the main feature, the Royal Gorge Bridge, remained mostly unscathed, and the community rallied to bring it back even better than before.

Today, visitors should start with a walk across the historic bridge, which, at 955 feet above the Arkansas River, is the highest bridge in the country. After that, see the gorge from the air either within an aerial gondola or by the zip line—also the highest in the country—and let younger kids release some energy in the three-story adventure playland. And be sure not to miss seeing the mini-documentary on the bridge's ninety-year history, shown in the theater.

Royal Gorge Bridge & Park, 4218 County Rd. 3A, Cañon City
888-333-5597, royalgorgebridge.com

TIP

Although Royal Gorge Bridge & Park is open 365 days a year, weather permitting, be sure to check the website for the hours of operation for the visitor center, bridge, theater, and playland. Note also that the park has longer hours from late May through August and shorter hours from late October through early March.

MINE FOR FUN
IN CRIPPLE CREEK

The bright red, blue, and yellow paint of the Cripple Creek and Victor Narrow Gauge Railroad's Engine No. 2 might bring about visions of Thomas the Tank Engine, but there's nothing imagined about this century-old steam locomotive. Doctor and railroad family man John Birmingham opened the CC&VNGR in 1967, and family members have been chugging visitors on forty-minute, four-mile excursions south of Cripple Creek and back ever since.

The railroad is just one historic attraction to be found among the numerous casinos that also call the area home. The hour-long tour at the Mollie Kathleen Gold Mine, the first to be discovered and claimed by a woman back in 1891, begins with donning a hard hat and descending a thousand-foot shaft below ground and ends with a free gold ore sample.

At Butte Theatre, heroes and villains accept cheers and boos from the audience for their roles in traditional melodramas—which have been running here more than seventy years. And four museums (and two more in nearby Victor) explore everything from the outlaws to the madams of Cripple Creek's early days.

The folks at the Cripple Creek Heritage and Information Center will gladly help you figure out what you'll most enjoy visiting. What's more, the center offers the most stunning views of the town and the Sangre de Cristo Mountains alongside its many educational exhibits.

Cripple Creek
visitcripplecreek.com

TIP

It's not unusual to see cars (or people) wandering a bit aimlessly around town searching for donkeys. Believed to be descendants of those that originally worked the mines during the Gold Rush, the local herd of fourteen is free-roaming by city ordinance from mid-May through mid-October. Rumor has it, if the high school is in session, the donkeys can often be found grazing there, weekdays around lunchtime, though money for regular feed and care is raised through the annual Donkey Derby Days festival held in June.

PLAY AND STAY
IN BUENA VISTA

The small mountain town of Buena Vista, a longtime home base for outdoor enthusiasts, has really come into its own since 2013. The growth can be seen most downtown and along South Main Street, where new and renovated shops, restaurants, and parks abound.

Whether you spend a day or a few nights, or come to soak for a few hours in the nearby Mt. Princeton Hot Springs, plan to be welcomed by this friendly community. Order a breakfast burrito and a Moroccan latte at The Buena Vista Roastery Café, sip a whiskey cocktail at Deerhammer Distilling Company, and find that perfect souvenir or gift at CKS Main Street, Rock Paper Scissors, or The Village.

Buena Vista Chamber of Commerce & Visitor Center
buenavistacolorado.org

TIP

The first thing you should know when visiting Buena Vista is how to say the town's name correctly. It's "BEW-na Vista," *not* the Spanish pronunciation, "BWAY-na Vista." Town founders back in 1879 chose to give the word an Americanized pronunciation, patterning it after the word *beautiful.* If the full name doesn't roll off your tongue, it's perfectly OK to call the town *Bewnie* or *BV.*

Mt. Princeton Hot Springs
15870 County Rd. 162, Nathrop
719-395-2447, mtprinceton.com

The Buena Vista Roastery Café
409 E. Main St., Buena Vista
719-966-5500, bvroasterycafe.com

Deerhammer Distilling Company
321 E. Main St., Buena Vista
719-395-9464, deerhammer.com

CKS Main Street
327 E. Main St., Buena Vista
719-395-9206, cksmainstreet.com

Rock Paper Scissors
411 E. Main St., Buena Vista
720-300-2051, rockpaperscissorscreative.com

The Village
414 E. Main St., Buena Vista
719-966-5322, thevillagebv.com

RAFT THE ARKANSAS RIVER
WITH THE ECHO CANYON FOLKS

There's nothing like a day on the river, with blue skies and fluffy white clouds above, and smooth waters below—except a day on the river, bouncing around in class III to class V rapids, getting splashed in the face, and laughing the whole time.

Whichever whitewater rafting experience sounds better to you, the folks at Echo Canyon River Expeditions are happy to oblige. They've guided trips on the Arkansas River waters since 1978 and can train you in all the paddling skills you'll need. When you're done, however, the soggy shorts stuck to your bum and the water spots on your sunglasses will be yours to manage.

Echo Canyon River Expeditions
45000 W. US Hwy. 50, Cañon City
800-755-3246, raftecho.com

TIP

Though Echo Canyon River Expeditions is only an hour drive from Colorado Springs, in 2017, the professional outfitters opened up a new side to the business that you might want to try. Royal Gorge Cabins (royalgorgecabins.com), overlooking the Sangre de Cristo Mountains, offers single and double king-bed luxury cabins with indoor/outdoor fireplaces as well as single and double queen-bed glamping tents with sweet fire rings. Why not spend a night or two and make a stop at Royal Gorge Park (No. 85) as well—for a purely Colorado adventure?

89

GET ACTIVE
IN SALIDA

The best place in Colorado to climb a fourteener (or two or three) is the Upper Arkansas River Valley's Chaffee County because hikers can choose from fourteen of these high-elevation peaks. And one of the best places for outdoor enthusiasts of all sorts to make a home base in Chaffee County is Salida, about a two-hour drive from Colorado Springs.

The activities in Salida are endless—from world-class rafting and kayaking to rock hounding, four-wheeling, and mountain biking. At seventy years and counting, America's oldest whitewater festival, FIBArk (aka First in Boating on the Arkansas), draws paddlers and spectators from throughout the world every June for four days of river competitions and related community events.

But Salida isn't only for outdoor junkies. It's also home to the largest historic downtown district in the state. You'll find a wide range of dining options, such as local favorite Amica's Pizza & Microbrewery, as well as eclectic shops and an extensive art community. And if you'll visit in June, catch the Salida Art Walk, a three-day event during which local artists open up their studios and offer demonstrations of their work.

Salida, Colorado
salida.com

HOWL
WITH THE WOLVES IN DIVIDE

Each wolf at the Colorado Wolf and Wildlife Center has a story, and because this is as much an educational facility as a rescue, tour guides share them. Timber wolves Kwahadi and Zaltana survived a backyard breeder who planned to sell them to the general public. Amarok, another Timber, was found roaming the streets of Colombia, where wolves are not native, so it's believed he was part of the illegal wildlife trade. All three can be seen during multiple, reservation-required, daily tours, Tuesday through Sunday, along with Arctic wolves, coyotes, and fox. Just make sure to connect with your inner wolf before visiting. All tours end with a group howl—and if you're lucky, the pack will join in.

Colorado Wolf and Wildlife Center
4729 Twin Rocks Rd., Divide
719-687-9742, wolfeducation.org

Credit: KK Creative Co

SHOPPING AND FASHION

SHOP THE LARGEST ANTIQUE MALL IN THE STATE

With sixty-five thousand square feet of space and more than three hundred vendors, American Classics Marketplace is Colorado's largest antique mall. Getting lost is easy—trust me—so the smartest thing you can do is grab a map at the front door.

You may *think* you'll remember which classic celebrity-named aisle you just finished, but you won't. You'll be distracted by the vintage Dictaphone at one booth, the sunflower-yellow Fiestaware sugar bowl you need to complete your collection at another, or John Denver's *Rocky Mountain High* album peeking out from the corner of a third.

American Classics Marketplace
1815 N. Academy Blvd., Colorado Springs
719-596-8585, americanclassicsmarketplace.com

TREAT YOURSELF AND OTHERS

AT THE TRADING POST

Need a Colorado Springs–themed T-shirt, water bottle, hat, or keychain? Or perhaps a handmade Native American turquoise necklace? Look no further than Garden of the Gods Trading Post, tucked in at the southwest edge of the park in Manitou Springs.

The trading post is the largest gift shop in the Pikes Peak region, as well as the oldest in the state, with an opening date of April 7, 1929. But before digging into the racks, stacks, and shelves to find the perfect gift, check out the display of historical photos and artifacts at the back of the store. You'll learn the story of founder Charles Strausenback and how his passion for both souvenirs and Southwestern art became the shopping experience you're enjoying today.

Garden of the Gods Trading Post
324 Beckers Ln., Manitou Springs
719-685-9045, gardenofthegodstradingpost.com

93

HUNT FOR TREASURES
IN OLD COLORADO CITY

Merchants took up residence in Old Colorado City more than one hundred years ago during the Pikes Peak Gold Rush, and merchants still thrive in this quaint historic district. Almost ten dozen boutiques, galleries, and restaurants offer up their goods here, so it's easy to spend a few hours—or days, for shopaholics—wandering and window shopping.

Stop in Chavez Gallery for the fun surrealist art of locals Liese and Kris Chavez. Peruse the cases of fine jewelry and other art at the Squash Blossom. Discover unique women's clothing, accessories, and gifts at EllyBlue, a boutique named for the owner's one-blue-eyed dog Elly. And if you want to take home a treat or squeaky toy for your own dog (or cat), hit up Republic of Paws.

Keep in mind that although most shops in Old Colorado City are located on Colorado Avenue between Twenty-Fourth Street and Twenty-Ninth Street, there are not-to-be-missed outliers, such as award-winning women's clothing and accessories shop Eve's Revolution.

Old Colorado City Shopping District
shopoldcoloradocity.com

Chavez Gallery
2524½ W. Colorado Ave., Colorado Springs
719-963-6925, chavezartgallery.com

Squash Blossom
2531 W. Colorado Ave., Colorado Springs
719-632-1899, squashblossom.com

EllyBlue
2605 W. Colorado Ave., Colorado Springs
719-520-0556, ellybluecos.com

Republic of Paws
2411 W. Colorado Ave., Colorado Springs
719-634-5139, republicofpaws.com

Eve's Revolution
1312 W. Colorado Ave., Colorado Springs
719-633-1357, evesrevolution.com

SEEK OUT SOUVENIRS AND MORE IN MANITOU SPRINGS

The tourist looking for a huge range of Pikes Peak T-shirts, ball caps, and water bottles won't be disappointed in Manitou Springs. But tucked among the souvenir stores are lots of top-notch locally owned galleries and boutiques that are sure to appeal to visitors looking for original artwork, one-of-a-kind fashions, and unique gifts for the folks at home.

Do some exploring on your own while seeking out Green Horse Gallery, with works from more than fifty artists, seven of whom are locals who share management of the gallery. La Henna Boheme is where you'll find boho women's clothing, gifts, and henna body art. Southwest Silver Company is one of the best-priced rock, crystal, and fossil shops in town. And Pikes Peak Chocolate and Ice Cream is where to head for handmade sweet treats and scoops of Josh & John's (see No. 14), while Radiantly Raw is the place to go for organic raw chocolates.

Green Horse Gallery
729 Manitou Ave., Manitou Springs
719-685-0636, greenhorsegallery.com

La Henna Boheme
801 Manitou Ave., Manitou Springs
719-636-2626, facebook.com/pg/LaHennaBoheme

Southwest Silver Co.
952 Manitou Ave., Manitou Springs
719-685-9197, facebook.com/pg/southwestsilvercompany

Pikes Peak Chocolate and Ice Cream
805 Manitou Ave., Manitou Springs
719-685-9600, pikespeakchocolate.com

Radiantly Raw
116 Cañon Ave., Manitou Springs
719-749-6176, radiantlyrawkitchen.com

TIP

Labor Day heralds the best weekend of the summer in Manitou Springs for arts and crafts enthusiasts. The Commonwheel Artists Annual Art Festival, a juried event hosted by the Commonwheel Artists Co-Op (commonwheel.com) has become a hometown favorite, bringing together one hundred-plus jewelers, potters, photographers, sculptors, painters, and more for more than forty years.

MAKE THESE DOWNTOWN SHOPS
A MUST-STOP

Downtown Colorado Springs along and in the side streets just off Tejon Street is overflowing with the storefronts of great shops and galleries, and many of the top tier have served locals and tourists for decades.

Any serious shopper's stop list should include Terra Verde and Colorado Co-Op for women's clothing, accessories, and home goods; Sparrow Hawk for kitchen and cooking needs; Mountain Chalet for outdoor gear; and Escape Velocity for comic and graphic novels. And one of the newer not-to-miss stops is Ladyfingers Letterpress, where wife-and-wife team Arley-Rose Torsone and Morgan Calderini design and print quirky greeting cards, which they sell alongside other gift-worthy local artist products.

Terra Verde
208 N. Tejon St., Colorado Springs
719-444-8621, terraverdestyle.com

Colorado Co-Op
315 N. Tejon St., Colorado Springs
719-389-0696, facebook.com/coloradocoop

Sparrow Hawk
120 N. Tejon St., Colorado Springs
719-471-3235, sparrowhawkcookware.com

Mountain Chalet
226 N. Tejon St., Colorado Springs
719-633-0732, mtnchalet.com

Escape Velocity Comics & Graphic Novels
19 E. Bijou St., Colorado Springs
719-578-8847, escapevelocitycomics.com

Ladyfingers Letterpress
113 E. Bijou St., Colorado Springs
401-523-3087, ladyfingersletterpress.com

STOCK UP
AT ANNA'S APOTHECARY

Clear glass jars full of dried herbs and teas line one full wall of Anna's Apothecary. Handmade tinctures, elixirs, perfumes, candles, and bitters fill out other shelves and tables. All of these items were concocted by herbalist Anna Papini and permaculturist Sara Berry, sisters who grew up in nearby Florissant, Colorado.

The apothecary is a veritable playground for folks seeking natural, organic, and non-GMO products to help with physical and emotional healing, seasonal ailments, and skin care. For even more play, sign up for an Anna's Apothecary workshop, ranging from local medicinal herb walks and make-your-own bitters classes to moon alchemy sessions that include developing lunar-connected herbal remedies and discussing new- and full-moon rituals.

Anna's Apothecary
116 Cañon Ave., Manitou Springs
719-685-2260, annasapothecary.com

CONSIDER CONSUMING

COLORADO'S LEGAL CANNABIS

Private consumption of cannabis for those twenty-one and older has been legal in Colorado since December 2012, and retail sales began January 1, 2014, for locals and tourists alike. Although voters approved the constitutional amendment, individual localities can still opt to ban recreational sales. Both Colorado Springs and unincorporated El Paso County made that choice, but neighboring Manitou Springs chose differently, and today there are two recreational shops in the city.

Emerald Fields and Maggie's Farm, which sit less than half a mile apart on Manitou Avenue near Highway 24, are easily identified by their often-overflowing parking lots during business hours. Each has its own vibe. Emerald Fields feels like a boutique; Maggie's Farm feels more industrial. Whichever you choose, bring cash or an ATM card, and don't hesitate to ask anything of the knowledgeable budtenders you'll find at both.

Emerald Fields
27 Manitou Ave., Manitou Springs
719-375-0554, emeraldfields.com

Maggie's Farm
141 Manitou Ave., Manitou Springs
719-685-1655, maggiesfarmmarijuana.com

SOOTHE A SWEET TOOTH
AT PATSY'S

The scent of fresh popcorn fills your nose upon arrival at the original Patsy's Candies location up the hill on Twenty-First Street, and samples of house-made truffles, caramel corn, and salt water taffy greet you upon entry.

Since 1902, Patsy's candy makers have been forming and drenching chocolates, pulling and stretching taffy, and coating that aforementioned popped corn with pure butterscotch. These days, curious customers can watch the process from behind clear-glass windows. Farther west in Manitou Springs, Patsy's not only sells the same treats, but is itself a treat to visit as the only permanent open-air concession stand in the state. (Just try to get the kids past these displays!)

Patsy's Candies
1540 S. Twenty-First St., Colorado Springs, 719-633-7215
930 Manitou Ave., Manitou Springs, 719-685-9437
patsyscandies.com

99

GO VINTAGE
AT THE LEECHPIT

The originator of the "Keep Colorado Springs Lame" campaign, the Leechpit sells the tongue-firmly-in-cheek tagline on stickers, T-shirts, and patches, and has even upgraded the basic text-only black-and-white version to a fancy, colorful mountain design. It is, however, one of the few new things that owners Adam and Heather Leech sell at their fifteen-year-old business.

Most of the display space in the carefully organized but packed front-door-to-back westside shop is filled with rare records, tapes, and CDs; vintage toys, games, and lunchboxes; and a whole variety of twentieth-century clothing, shoes, and jewelry. One other intriguing find here? Hobo Nickels, with designs ranging from *Simpsons* characters to Nikola Tesla, each hand-carved and hawked by Adam.

Leechpit
3020 W. Colorado Ave., Suite A, Colorado Springs
719-634-DORK (3675), leechpit.com

100

BROWSE
COLORADO SPRINGS' USED BOOKSTORES

Booker and Pages, the house cats at Bargain Book Warehouse, may or may not greet customers at the door. It depends if they're feeling curious or napping in the stacks. Same for Gray and Blue, the felines that call The Bookman home.

Not every used bookstore in Colorado Springs keeps cats on staff—Hooked On Books, Books for You, and Poor Richard's Bookstore, for instance. All of them, however, offer great deals on thousands upon thousands of hardcovers and paperbacks across all genres, and most have been doing business in this community for more than thirty years.

Bargain Book Warehouse
104 W. Cucharras St., Colorado Springs
719-475-8091, facebook.com/Bargain-Book-Warehouse-188430329872

The Bookman
631 Colorado Ave., Colorado Springs
719-636-0055, facebook.com/thebookmanlives

Hooked On Books
3918 Maizeland Rd., Colorado Springs, 719-596-1621
10 E. Bijou St., Colorado Springs, 719-419-7660
hookedonbooksco.com

Books for You
1737 S. Eighth St., Colorado Springs
719-630-0502, booksforyou.us

Poor Richard's Bookstore
320 N. Tejon St., Colorado Springs
719-578-5549, poorrichardsdowntown.com

Cave of the Winds Via Feratta
(Courtesy Pikes Peak Country Attractions)

SUGGESTED ITINERARIES

FOR ART LOVERS

Engage in Innovative Arts at Green Box, 49

Go AWOL at the Ent Center for the Arts, 35

See Art, Make Art, Live Art at the FAC, 42

Check Out Art on the Streets, 36

Share in the Shenanigans On and Off the First Friday Shuttle, 39

FOR KIDS (OF ALL AGES)

Shred Memorial Park Skate Park, 58

Blast into the Past at the Manitou Springs Penny Arcade, 102

Choose Your Own Museum Adventure, 98

Ask the Big Questions at the What IF… Festival, 41

Dig into Cave of the Winds, 91

FOR THOSE PLANNING A DATE NIGHT

Soak at SunWater Spa, 74

Enjoy Dinner and a Movie Under the Stars at Margarita at Pine Creek, 4

View a Film at Kimball's Peak Three, 40

Learn to Boot Scoot and Two-Step at Cowboy's, 34

Shimmy on Over to a Peaks and Pasties Performance, 47

Get Starry-Eyed with the Astronomical Society, 78

FOR THOSE WHO LOVE ALL CRITTERS AND CREATURES

FOR HISTORY BUFFS

FOR HIKERS

Colorado Springs Fine Arts Center at Colorado College *(Credit: Phillip Spears)*

Cripple Creek and Victor Narrow Gauge Railroad
(Courtesy Pikes Peak Country Attractions)

ACTIVITIES BY SEASON

SPRING

SUMMER

FALL

WINTER

INDEX